TIPS FOR TEACHERS

Hundreds of Quick, Innovative Strategies to
Ignite and Deepen Learning

English Language Arts

IncentivePublications

BY WORLD BOOK
a Scott Fetzer company

CONTENTS

A Dynamic Little Handbook

Great Tips for English Language Arts Students, Administrators, Teachers, and Parents

"Wow! There is so much great information here; I have to have this on my bookshelf!" Teachers, school administrators, and parents have repeatedly said this when they've scanned any of the tips compiled in this dynamic little handbook!

Tips for Teachers: English Language Arts pulls together a wealth of assistance for instruction in an at-your-fingertips format. Ten chapters present helpful teaching tips, each chapter prepared by a different expert author well versed in a specific content area. You'll find such materials used as workshop handouts, professional development tools, and treasured resources for beginning and advanced educators alike. Each chapter is packed with research-based and practical information, advice, instructional strategies, student project ideas, graphic organizers, and creative activities on various educational and curriculum-related topics.

Keep this reference handbook, and others in this series, at the ready—you'll reach for them often no matter what content area you teach! That's right! This handbook is not only for English or Language Arts teachers. Page through each handbook and learn how to integrate language arts and literacy instruction into any classroom.

Ideas Spanning the Language Arts

Ten chapters offer hundreds of tips across the strands of English language arts. You'll quickly see the depth and quality of the tips for close reading of literary and informational texts, text analysis and evaluation, writing, vocabulary use and development, argumentation, speaking, listening, researching, integrating language arts curriculum models, podcasting, and planning for presentations and projects. The possibilities for integrating all of these strands, expertly woven throughout the tips, are countless.

Ample Possibilities for Differentiation

Teachers and learners praise this collection of language arts tips for the rich variety of innovative and effective practices. They love the inherent support for differentiated instruction. In every chapter, a variety of options is offered for approaches to learning; for materials, tools, and modalities; for student feedback; for assessment; and for teacher feedback. The use of technology in the classroom (from simple to complex) explodes the number of possibilities. There are plenty of avenues for every student to learn.

Top-Notch Authors

Different authors—each with plenty of expertise to offer—contributed to this volume. Many of them have earned national recognition as educational writers and speakers. All are seasoned teachers who have used these suggestions in their classrooms. Others are educational consultants, administrators, or teacher trainers who have honed their suggestions through years of conversing and working with educators, parents, and students. Their combined wealth of understanding and involvement with language arts skills, concepts, and standards combines to create a dynamic compendium of creative, well-tested, student-friendly practices.

Included Authors:

Dr. Sharon Faber
Marjorie Frank
Joy MacKenzie
Dr. Bill McBride
Peri Sandifer
Sandra Schurr
Dedra Stafford

Support for College- and Career-Ready Standards

This book is an excellent tool for strengthening any college- and career-readiness curriculum. Whether your state is committed to Common Core or another set of educational standards, this volume offers guidance and support in reaching English language arts standards. The content reflects seriousness about the depth and rigor needed in student learning. You'll find lively and workable ways to guide students to deep analysis of texts, broader understanding of vocabulary, higher-level writing skills, stronger preparation and presentation of ideas in writing and speaking, and better use and knowledge of their language. You'll love the inspiration that adds zest to your teaching of the language arts—while you help your students meet whatever standards serve as your guide. (Pages 12 through 18 show how the contents connect with the Common Core State Standards for Language Arts in grades 6 through 12.)

Ignite Learning with Technology

Technology and language arts learning are natural partners to enhance student learning and help students master essential classroom skills. Connections between tips content and technology applications are addressed in the introduction to each chapter. Chapters 7, **Log On and Inspire Savvy Internet Research and Evaluation**, and 10, **Podcast Your Way to Integrated Learning**, are heavily technology dependent. In addition, **Technology Connections,** on pages 8 through 11, gives some suggestions for integrating technology into language arts lessons, activities, and explorations. Since technology is ever-changing, these tips will help get you into the habit of seeing how future technologies can be incorporated into daily learning!

How to Use This Book

This book is organized by language arts strand or topic. Each chapter has these key features:

- an introduction to teaching and learning related to the topic
- a variety of explanations, strategies, information, lists, steps, and/or how-to instructions specific to the topic
- student pages for use in one or several activities

Although the tips are grouped by topic within the language arts, the chapters are not meant to segregate ideas or language arts topics. As you use this book, you will see that strategies from each chapter spill over into other chapters and mix dynamically. Many strategies fit several chapters, and the tips in any one chapter give hearty support to the ideas in others.

For example:

- Vocabulary (Chapter 1) is foundational to reading, writing, and speaking, so the tips in Chapter 1 will be welcome as you work with all the other topics (Chapters 1 through 10).
- Tips for Internet Research (Chapter 7) make use of reading strategies (Chapter 2) and will offer plenty of opportunities for text analysis (Chapter 3), writing (Chapters 4 and 5), speech preparation (Chapter 6), argumentative speaking or writing (Chapters 4, 5, and 6), and for the preparation of research papers, projects, or podcasts (Chapters 8, 9, and 10).
- Tips for Writing (Chapter 4) are invaluable for speeches and discussions (Chapters 5 and 6), Internet evaluation (Chapter 7), research papers (Chapter 8), and many student projects, products, and podcasts (Chapter 10).
- Reading and writing strategies (Chapters 2, 3, and 4) will come in handy with skills honed through strategies in every other chapter.

Technology Connections

Technology is ubiquitous. It affects the lives of students and teachers in dozens of ways every day. As digital natives, students need teachers who will step beyond the way they were taught and into a classroom bustling with possibilities for transmitting, developing, and assessing skills. Students want more options for learning. They want to explore and express their understanding of new content by connecting it to real-world tools that they know and love. For authentic learning in the real world, technology must have a strong presence in the classroom. And be mindful that some digital natives know everything and more about, say, texting, but next to nothing about getting beyond Google™ and assessing the validity and suitability of individual websites.

To incorporate technology in the classroom, be sure to follow your school policies and guidelines for Internet safety and etiquette, technology use, and communication with students and parents. Your technology-connection plans will be greatly affected by the school's practices, restrictions, platforms, software, hardware, approved websites, and overall access to technology.

In addition to helping students acquire skills they need to thrive in a highly technological culture, effective use of technology in the classroom inspires and facilitates

- intellectual challenge
- curiosity and creativity
- interaction and collaboration
- independent learning
- decision making
- analysis and synthesis
- desire to problem solve
- need for deeper understanding
- global connections
- wider feedback
- differentiation
- engagement with learning experiences
- excitement about ideas and information
- involvement with real-life issues

So don't ban those little ear buds! Digital devices have a place in your classroom. Students crave them, use them, and are motivated to learn with them. **They** know how to work the devices; **you** need to show them how to use the devices to learn the language arts concepts you want to teach. Here are a few tips for increasing meaningful, workable technology connections:

- Stretch yourself! Set goals to expand the use of technology in language arts lessons, projects, assignments, presentations, and assessments.

- Search out the best Internet sites and tools. Identify good sites, ideas, software options, and strategies to fit your particular needs and students.

- Expand appropriate use of social media. Use it for instructional and assessment tasks and to speed up communication with students and parents.

- Use as many kinds of software, hardware, platforms, and programs as you can to offer technology connections that support and enhance student learning and assessment.

- Look beyond the desktop, laptop, and tablet. Make use of other technology, from simple to sophisticated, such as cell phones, DVD and CD players, audio recorders, videocams, videogames, audio and video clips, digital cameras, webcams, clickers, digital whiteboards, MP3 players, electronic keyboards, and many others.

- Master and use available school-wide platforms or subscription programs.

- Watch for ways that technology can make learning relevant and appealing to individuals with different abilities or learning anxieties. A tech tool can dissolve barriers for reluctant learners, students studying English as a second language, or those who struggle with reading, writing, or speaking.

With technology's ever-changing platforms, keep up to date on the new and up-and-coming devices on the horizon. The ideas on pages 10 and 11 can be merged, adapted, and formatted to fit the specific digital platform you choose, now and in the future!

Sample Ideas for Language Arts Technology Connections

Teachers can:

- Create a classroom Twitter® account with a class-specific hashtag, and ask students to "follow" the account. Students can then tweet to the account using that hashtag. This educational Twitter will facilitate digital interaction between you and the students.

- Make assessments on PowerPoint® (or another presentation program). Create some questions that require students to process information visually.

- Tweet or text quiz questions to students for a quick, formative assessment.

- Put assignments on email or social media sites.

- Create a board on Pinterest® or other posting website to introduce works of literature, give sentences to rework, or offer tips for test preparation.

- Tweet or email reminders of due dates for assignments.

- Ask students to tweet or text instant feedback to a presentation. (Give specific direction, such as: "What reason in this essay was most supportive of the speaker's viewpoint?")

- Create QR codes to send students on a scavenger hunt. Students scan the codes and follow clues to find information for a reading or writing assignment.

- Collect Instagram™ images and use them as prompts for writing and discussion.

- Ask students to tweet questions about concepts, lessons, or assignments that they don't understand. Use the questions to plan for reteaching or to clarify information.

Students can:

- Summarize almost any assignment, story, lecture, paragraph, argument (for or against something), article, video, speech, or movie with a tweet or text. Use the 140-character format of Twitter to create and share short stories, poems, or serialized texts.

- Turn writing into multimedia experiences with free multimedia tools. Animate short stories, combine slides of supporting examples with argumentative writing, or film scenes (with a smart phone, tablet, or video camera) to enhance poetry.

- Find a website where students can create a step-by-step graphic organizer guide to analyze and evaluate a speech. Use the guide to evaluate a speech found online.

- Change the informal communication in a text message or tweet to a full sentence or paragraph written formally.

- Use a digital camera to create photo vocabulary cards or concept cards for teaching or review.

- Track a hashtag or follow an issue on Twitter. Keep notes for a group discussion.

- Video a field trip and text written captions to accompany video clips.

- Prepare "Book Talks" (or "Movie Talks," "Video Clip Talks," or talks about concepts that are read, listened to, or viewed). Record these on a podcast.

- Take on the persona of a character from a literary work or an actual person in history. Make video recordings of one another telling each character's story in dramatizations or monologues.

- Read a selection of Internet articles that support (or disagree with) a particular position on an issue. Use a cell phone to text a "vote" (like voting for a contestant on such a TV show as *American Idol)* for the article that "wins" (does the best job of making the point with reliable evidence and logical argument).

- Work with a group to create criteria for analyzing or critiquing the messages from songs. Apply the criteria to one or more popular songs, accessed digitally.

- Write a script and create a video clip to demonstrate or explain how to use a particular technological tool.

- Set up a debate where two or more writers (or speakers) make claims and counter-claims. Publish a text or audio file of an argument on a wiki. Other participants can rate the debate.

- Create jingles, raps, or short songs to teach math facts, vocabulary words, spelling, or any concept (such as photosynthesis, palindromic numbers, or democracy). Use a cell phone camera to record and share the creations.

- Perform an Internet grammar hunt. Find examples online of a particular grammatical structure (such as adverbial clauses or compound-complex sentences).

- Skype™ with another class at another location in the world to share recommendations or comments about a play, song, TV show, book, event, or idea.

- Use a free service like Google Drive™ to collaborate on writing assignments. Join with students from other classes to work together, give feedback, and polish written projects.

- Find a website for creating rubrics. Work in pairs or small groups to design a rubric for evaluating a speech, poem, dramatization, or any other written or spoken text.

- Create a visual template to use for mapping and comparing messages from TV ads.

- Use a digital camera to document the process of writing an essay, preparing a speech, researching an issue, or completing a project.

- Use Twitter to create a progressive story, poem, essay, or character.

- Use survey software (such as Survey Monkey®) to take a class survey. Record, examine, and write a written analysis of the data.

Standards Connections

Common Core State Standards for Reading, Grades 6-12

Anchor Standard	Corresponding Grade-Level Standards	Standard	Pages that Support
Key Ideas and Details			
CCRA.R.1	RL.6-8.1; RL.9-10.1; RL.11-12.1; RI.6-8.1; RI.9-10.1; RI.11-12.1; RH.6-8.1; RH.9-10.1; RH.11-12.1; RST.6-8.1; RST.9-10.1; RST.11.12.1	Read closely to determine what the text says explicitly and to make logical inferences from it; cite specific textual evidence when writing or speaking to support conclusions drawn from the text.	Ch 2: 28-41 Ch 3: 42-50 Ch 4: 51-65 Ch 6: 76-86 Ch 7: 87-97 Ch 8: 98-109 Ch 9: 110-125 Ch 10: 126-134
CCRA.R.2	RL.6-8.2; RL.9-10.2; RL.11-12.2; RI.6-8.2; RI.9-10.2; RI.11-12.2; RH.6-8.2; RH.9-10.2; RH.11-12.2; RST.6-8.2; RST.9-10.2; RST.11.12.2	Determine central ideas or themes of a text and analyze their development; summarize the key supporting details and ideas.	Ch 2: 28-41 Ch 3: 42-50 Ch 4: 51-65 Ch 6: 76-86 Ch 7: 87-97 Ch 8: 98-109 Ch 9: 110-125 Ch 10: 126-134
CCRA.R.3	RL.6-8.3; RL.9-10.3; RL.11-12.3; RI.6-8.3; RI.9-10.3; RI.11-12.3; RH.6-8.3; RH.9-10.3; RH.11-12.3; RST.6-8.3; RST.9-10.3; RST.11.12.3	Analyze how and why individuals, events, and ideas develop and interact over the course of a text.	Ch 2: 28-47 Ch 3: 42-50 Ch 6: 76-86 Ch 7: 87-97 Ch 8: 98-109 Ch 9: 110-125
Craft and Structure			
CCRA.R.4	RL.6-8.4; RL.9-10.4; RL.11-12.4; RI.6-8.4; RI.9-10.4; RI.11-12.4; RH.6-8.4; RH.9-10.4; RH.11-12.4; RST.6-8.4; RST.9-10.4; RST.11.12.4	Interpret words and phrases as they are used in a text, including determining technical, connotative, and figurative meanings, and analyze how specific word choices shape meaning or tone.	Ch 1: 19-27 Ch 2: 28-47 Ch 3: 42-50 Ch 4: 51-65 Ch 6: 76-86 Ch 9: 110-125
CCRA.R.5	RL.6-8.5; RL.9-10.5; RL.11-12.5; RI.6-8.5; RI.9-10.5; RI.11-12.5; RH.6-8.5; RH.9-10.5; RH.11-12.5; RST.6-8.5; RST.9-10.5; RST.11.12.5	Analyze the structure of texts, including how specific sentences, paragraphs, and larger portions of the text (e.g., a section, chapter, scene, or stanza) relate to each other and the whole.	Ch 2: 28-47 Ch 3: 42-50 Ch 4: 51-65 Ch 6: 76-86 Ch 8: 98-109 Ch 9: 110-125

Anchor Standard	Corresponding Grade-Level Standards	Standard	Pages that Support
CCRA.R.6	RL.6-8.1; RL.9-10.1; RL.11-12.1; RI.6-8.1; RI.9-10.1; RI.11-12.1; RH.6-8.6; RH.9-10.6; RH.11-12.6; RST.6-8.6; RST.9-10.6; RST.11.12.6	Assess how point of view or purpose shapes the content and style of a text.	Ch 2: 28-47 Ch 3: 42-50 Ch 4: 51-65 Ch 6: 76-86 Ch 7: 87-97 Ch 9: 110-125
Integration of Knowledge and Ideas			
CCRA.R.7	RL.6-8.7; RL.9-10.7; RL.11-12.7; RI.6-8.7; RI.9-10.7; RI.11-12.7; RH.6-8.7; RH.9-10.7; RH.11-12.7; RST.6-8.7; RST.9-10.7; RST.11.12.7	Integrate and evaluate content presented in diverse media and formats, including visually and quantitatively, as well as in words.	Ch 2: 28-41 Ch 3: 42-50 Ch 4: 51-65 Ch 6: 76-86 Ch 7: 87-97 Ch 8: 98-109 Ch 9: 110-125 Ch 10: 126-134
CCRA.R.8	RL.6-8.8; RL.9-10.8; RL.11-12.8; RI.6-8.8; RI.9-10.1; RI.11-12.1; RH.6-8.8; RH.9-10.8; RH.11-12.8; RST.6-8.8; RST.9-10.8; RST.11.12.8	Delineate and evaluate the argument and specific claims in a text, including the validity of the reasoning as well as the relevance and sufficiency of the evidence.	Ch 2: 28-41 Ch 3: 42-50 Ch 4: 51-65 Ch 6: 76-86 Ch 7: 87-97 Ch 8: 98-109 Ch 9: 110-125 Ch 10: 126-134
CCRA.R.9	RL.6-8.9; RL.9-10.9; RL.11-12.9; RI.6-8.9; RI.9-10.9; RI.11-12.9; RH.6-8.9; RH.9-10.9; RH.11-12.9; RST.6-8.9; RST.9-10.9; RST.11.12.9	Analyze how two or more texts address similar themes or topics in order to build knowledge or to compare the approaches the authors take.	Ch 2: 28-41 Ch 3: 42-50 Ch 4: 51-65 Ch 6: 76-86 Ch 7: 87-97 Ch 8: 98-109 Ch 9: 110-125 Ch 10: 126-134
Range of Reading and Level of Text Complexity			
CCRA.R.10	RL.6-8.10; RL.9-10.10; RL.11-12.10; RI.6-8.10; RI.9-10.10; RI.11-12.10; RH.9-10.10; RH.11-12.10; RST.6-8.10; RST.9-10.10; RST.11.12.10	Read and comprehend complex literary and informational texts independently and proficiently.	Ch 1: 19-27 Ch 2: 28-41 Ch 3: 42-50 Ch 4: 51-65 Ch 6: 76-86 Ch 7: 87-97 Ch 8: 98-109 Ch 9: 110-125

Common Core State Standards for Writing, Grades 6-12

Anchor Standard	Corresponding Grade-Level Standards	Standard	Pages that Support
Text Types and Purposes			
CCRA.W.1	W.6.1; W.7.1; W.8.1; W.9-10.1; W.11-12.1; WHST.6-8.1; WHST.9-10.1; WHST.11-12.1	Write arguments to support claims in an analysis of substantive topics or texts, using valid reasoning and relevant and sufficient evidence.	Ch 3: 42-50 Ch 4: 51-65 Ch 5: 66-75 Ch 6: 76-86 Ch 7: 87-97 Ch 8: 98-109 Ch 9: 110-125 Ch 10: 126-134
CCRA.W.2	W.6.2; W.7.2; W.8.2; W.9-10.2; W.11-12.2; WHST.6-8.2; WHST.9-10.2; WHST.11-12.2	Write informative/explanatory texts to examine and convey complex ideas and information clearly and accurately through the effective selection, organization, and analysis of content.	Ch 3: 42-50 Ch 4: 51-65 Ch 5: 66-75 Ch 6: 76-86 Ch 7: 87-97 Ch 8: 98-109 Ch 9: 110-125 Ch 10: 126-134
CCRA.W.3	W.6.3; W.7.3; W.8.3 W.9-10.3; W.11-12.3; WHST.6-8.3; WHST.9-10.3; WHST.11-12.3	Write narratives to develop real or imagined experiences or events using effective technique, well-chosen details, and well-structured event sequences.	Ch 3: 42-50 Ch 4: 51-65 Ch 9: 110-125 Ch 10: 126-134
Production and Distribution of Writing			
CCRA.W.4	W.6.4; W.7.4; W.8.4 W.9-10.4; W.11-12.4; WHST.6-8.4; WHST.9-10.4; WHST.11-12.4	Produce clear and coherent writing in which the development, organization, and style are appropriate to task, purpose, and audience.	Ch 4: 51-65 Ch 5: 66-75 Ch 7: 87-97 Ch 8: 98-109 Ch 9: 110-125 Ch 10: 126-134
CCRA.W.5	W.6.5; W.7.5; W.8.5 W.9-10.5; W.11-12.5; WHST.6-8.5; WHST.9-10.5; WHST.11-12.5	Develop and strengthen writing as needed by planning, revising, editing, rewriting, or trying a new approach.	Ch 4: 51-65 Ch 5: 66-75 Ch 7: 87-97 Ch 8: 98-109 Ch 9: 110-125 Ch 10: 126-134

Anchor Standard	Corresponding Grade-Level Standards	Standard	Pages that Support
CCRA.W.6	W.6.6; W.7.6; W.8.6 W.9-10.6; W.11-12.6; WHST.6-8.6; WHST.9-10.6; WHST.11-12.6	Use technology, including the Internet, to produce and publish writing and to interact and collaborate with others.	Ch 4: 51-65 Ch 5: 66-75 Ch 7: 87-97 Ch 8: 98-109 Ch 9: 110-125 Ch 10: 126-134
Research to Build and Present Knowledge			
CCRA.W.7	W.6.7; W.7.7; W.8.7 W.9-10.7; W.11-12.7; WHST.6-8.7; WHST.9-10.7; WHST.11-12.7	Conduct short as well as more sustained research projects based on focused questions, demonstrating understanding of the subject under investigation.	Ch 2: 28-41 Ch 3: 42-50 Ch 4: 51-65 Ch 5: 66-75 Ch 6: 76-86 Ch 7: 87-97 Ch 8: 98-109 Ch 9: 110-125 Ch 10: 126-134
CCRA.W.8	W.6.8; W.7.8; W.8.8 W.9-10.8; W.11-12.8; WHST.6-8.8; WHST.9-10.8; WHST.11-12.8	Gather relevant information from multiple print and digital sources, assess the credibility and accuracy of each source, and integrate the information while avoiding plagiarism.	Ch 2: 28-41 Ch 3: 42-50 Ch 4: 51-65 Ch 5: 66-75 Ch 6: 76-86 Ch 7: 87-97 Ch 8: 98-109 Ch 9: 110-125 Ch 10: 126-134
CCRA.W.9	W.6.9; W.7.9; W.8.9 W.9-10.9; W.11-12.9; WHST.6-8.9; WHST.9-10.9; WHST.11-12.9	Draw evidence from literary or informational texts to support analysis, reflection, and research.	Ch 2: 28-41 Ch 3: 42-50 Ch 4: 51-65 Ch 5: 66-75 Ch 6: 76-86 Ch 7: 87-97 Ch 8: 98-109 Ch 9: 110-125 Ch 10: 126-134

Anchor Standard	Corresponding Grade-Level Standards	Standard	Pages that Support
Range of Writing			
CCRA.W.10	W.6.10; W.7.10; W.8.10 W.9-10.10; W.11-12.10; WHST.6-8.10; WHST.9-10.10; WHST.11-12.10	Write routinely over extended time frames (time for research, reflection, and revision) and shorter time frames (a single sitting or a day or two) for a range of tasks, purposes, and audiences.	Ch 2: 28-41 Ch 3: 42-50 Ch 4: 51-65 Ch 5: 66-75 Ch 6: 76-86 Ch 7: 87-97 Ch 8: 98-109 Ch 9: 110-125 Ch 10: 126-134

Common Core State Standards for Speaking and Listening, Grades 6-12

Anchor Standard	Corresponding Grade-Level Standards	Standard	Pages that Support
Comprehension and Collaboration			
CCRA.SL.1	SL.6.1; SL.7.1; SL.8.1; SL.9-10.1; SL.11-12.1	Prepare for and participate effectively in a range of conversations and collaborations with diverse partners, building on others' ideas and expressing their own clearly and persuasively.	Ch 5: 66-75 Ch 6: 76-86 Ch 7: 87-97 Ch 9: 110-125 Ch 10: 126-134
CCRA.SL.2	SL.6.2; SL.7.2; SL.8.2; SL.9-10.2; SL.11-12.2	Integrate and evaluate information presented in diverse media and formats, including visually, quantitatively, and orally.	Ch 5: 66-75 Ch 6: 76-86 Ch 7: 87-97 Ch 9: 110-125 Ch 10: 126-134
CCRA.SL.3	SL.6.3; SL.7.3; SL.8.3; SL.9-10.3; SL.11-12.3	Evaluate a speaker's point of view, reasoning, and use of evidence and rhetoric.	Ch 5: 66-75 Ch 6: 76-86 Ch 7: 87-97 Ch 9: 110-125 Ch 10: 126-134

Anchor Standard	Corresponding Grade-Level Standards	Standard	Pages that Support
Presentation of Knowledge and Ideas			
CCRA.SL.4	SL.6.4; SL.7.4; SL.8.4; SL.9-10.4; SL.11-12.4	Present information, findings, and supporting evidence such that listeners can follow the line of reasoning and the organization, development, and style are appropriate to task, purpose, and audience.	Ch 5: 66-75 Ch 6: 76-86 Ch 7: 87-97 Ch 9: 110-125 Ch 10: 126-134
CCRA.SL.5	SL.6.5; SL.7.5; SL.8.5; SL.9-10.5; SL.11-12.5	Make strategic use of digital media and visual displays of data to express information and enhance understanding of presentations.	Ch 5: 66-75 Ch 6: 76-86 Ch 7: 87-97 Ch 9: 110-125 Ch 10: 126-134
CCRA.SL.6	SL.6.6; SL.7.6; SL.8.6; SL.9-10.6; SL.11-12.6	Adapt speech to a variety of contexts and communicative tasks, demonstrating command of formal English when indicated or appropriate.	Ch 5: 66-75 Ch 6: 76-86 Ch 7: 87-97 Ch 9: 110-125 Ch 10: 126-134

Common Core State Standards for Language, 6-12

Anchor Standard	Corresponding Grade-Level Standards	Standard	Pages that Support
Conventions of Standard English			
CCRA.L.1	L.6.1; L.7.1; L.8.1; L.9-10.1; L.11-12.1	Demonstrate command of the conventions of standard English grammar and usage when writing or speaking.	Ch 2: 28-41 Ch 3: 42-50 Ch 4: 51-65 Ch 5: 66-75 Ch 6: 76-86 Ch 7: 87-97 Ch 8: 98-109 Ch 9: 110-125 Ch 10: 126-134
CCRA.L.2	L.6.2; L.7.2; L.8.2; L.9-10.2; L.11-12.2	Demonstrate command of the conventions of standard English capitalization, punctuation, and spelling when writing.	Ch 2: 28-41 Ch 3: 42-50 Ch 4: 51-65 Ch 5: 66-75 Ch 6: 76-86 Ch 7: 87-97 Ch 8: 98-109 Ch 9: 110-125 Ch 10: 126-134

Anchor Standard	Corresponding Grade-Level Standards	Standard	Pages that Support
Knowledge of Language			
CCRA.L.3	L.6.3; L.7.3; L.8.3; L.9-10.3; L.11-12.3	Apply knowledge of language to understand how language functions in different contexts, to make effective choices for meaning or style, and to comprehend more fully when reading or listening.	Ch 1: 19-27 Ch 2: 28-41 Ch 3: 42-50 Ch 4: 51-65 Ch 5: 66-75 Ch 6: 76-86 Ch 7: 87-97 Ch 8: 98-109 Ch 9: 110-125 Ch 10: 126-134
Vocabulary Acquisition and Use			
CCRA.L.4	L.6.4; L.7.4; L.8.4; L.9-10.4; L.11-12.4	Determine or clarify the meaning of unknown and multiple-meaning words and phrases by using context clues, analyzing meaningful word parts, and consulting general and specialized reference materials, as appropriate.	Ch 1: 19-27 Ch 2: 28-41 Ch 3: 42-50 Ch 4: 51-65 Ch 8: 98-109
CCRA.L.5	L.6.5; L.7.5; L.8.5; L.9-10.5; L.11-12.5	Demonstrate understanding of figurative language, word relationships, and nuances in word meanings.	Ch 1: 19-27 Ch 2: 28-41 Ch 3: 42-50 Ch 4: 51-65
CCRA.L.6	L.6.6; L.7.6; L.8.6; L.9-10.6; L.11-12.6	Acquire and use accurately a range of general academic and domain-specific words and phrases sufficient for reading, writing, speaking, and listening at the college and career readiness level; demonstrate independence in gathering vocabulary knowledge when encountering an unknown term important to comprehension or expression.	Ch 1: 19-27 Ch 2: 28-41 Ch 3: 42-50 Ch 4: 51-65 Ch 5: 66-75 Ch 6: 76-86 Ch 7: 87-97 Ch 8: 98-109 Ch 9: 110-125 Ch 10: 126-134

Chapter 1
Make Vocabulary Unforgettable

Practical Tips for Helping Students
Build a Rich, Robust, and Lifelong Vocabulary

by Joy MacKenzie

Memorable Words

Rich, robust, and *unforgettable!* These terms describe the store of words secondary-level students need as they enter the adult world. Teachers know how critical a rich vocabulary is to student reading and writing success, as well as to the understanding of concepts in all content areas. We also know that a robust personal vocabulary contributes in all sorts of ways to success beyond school, to adeptness in social situations, and to personal satisfaction. However, students can hardly enjoy the benefits of rich, robust vocabularies if they can't remember the words! Make sure that the words you choose to teach are unforgettable!

Is that easier said than done? No! Scholarly research, teaching experience, and common sense tell us that we all are most likely to REALLY remember a new word when . . .

- it is connected to a visual representation, a strong emotion, or humor.
- it is connected to a rhythm or music.
- we hear and use the word in its different forms.
- we demonstrate the concept or meaning, or DO the process named by the word.
- we identify examples of the idea, description, or situation named by the word.
- we "map" the word to show its deeper meanings, connections, or implications.
- we use, share, expand, or apply the word using different forms of technology.
- we connect it to words, ideas, and events we already know.
- we think about causes, results, and implications of the idea named by the word.
- the word is taken apart so we can examine its parts.
- the word is associated with, compared to, and contrasted with other words that have similar (or different) structures, sounds, parts, or meanings.
- we experience multiple meanings or uses of the word.
- we use it as a part of our real-life means of communication, including social media.

Vocabulary Lived and Loved Is Vocabulary Learned

To build a strong vocabulary, fall in love with both the process and the product. Yes, it helps to know that a broad vocabulary contributes to success in all areas of life. But loving the learning of words is what "seals the deal" and guarantees results.

To help students live and love words . . .

Always...

- post words to be learned in a prominent place in the classroom, visible to all.

- take at least three to five minutes each day to do something with some of the words that reinforces their meanings and value in effective communication.

- present and demonstrate words in varied, multiple contexts. Engage students in this process, connecting the words to prior knowledge. Talk about when and where the words might be found in context or heard in conversation.

- connect the words to students' daily lives and to words they already know and use. Try to personalize this to individuals.

- address words using every "gateway" to the brain, appealing to as many senses and emotions as possible (e.g., sounds, touch sensations, surprise, joy, or anger).

- invite students to offer ideas that help them (and their classmates) "connect" other experiences and knowledge to a given word.

- use unexpected approaches and content to assess vocabulary learning. (See *Matching Is for Socks* on page 26.)

- remember that words are learned incrementally, through multiple exposures. Keep using words from previous lists.

- teach students a host of strategies for figuring out words they do not know (e.g., using context or structural analysis).

- congratulate students when they make use of previously learned words.

Never...

- think of yourself as a "teacher" of vocabulary. Rather, see yourself as the Pied Piper—gleeful, witty, or uproarious—leading an excited bunch of *abecedarians* on a scavenger hunt.

- stop thinking of ways to help students become fascinated with words. Make it a deeply ingrained habit in every content area and in every classroom moment.

- present vocabulary words as a list to be memorized for a test on Friday.

- ask students to learn more than 10 to 12 new vocabulary words at a time.

- be afraid to employ some outlandish, memorable approach to presenting a word (e.g., wearing odd clothing with objects attached to teach the words *outrageous*, *ragamuffin*, *preposterous*, or *vagabond*).

- present vocabulary by asking students to write each word multiple times, look up the meaning, and use it in a sentence. Such action is likely to create a loathing of vocabulary learning!

- stop with one exposure to a new word or one kind of activity per word.

- miss a chance to broaden students' understanding or use of a word.

- discourage students when they make use of words incorrectly. Instead, use this as a teachable moment to explain the correct usage.

- underestimate YOUR power in this process. The teacher's excitement about words and facility with words is one of the most powerful teaching strategies of all!

Surefire Strategies that Kindle Enthusiasm for Learning Vocabulary

Word Wall

No classroom should be without one! After a few weeks of school, students should have been exposed to enough interesting, useful, essential, energetic, and enigmatic words to create a "word wall." Select a committee in each class to choose the most fascinating or important words that have emerged (from any source) in class so far in the current school year. Then, set aside a time when the whole class is involved in the creation of the word wall to which words are added on a regular basis. If space is a problem, there is always the ceiling! Change words on the walls periodically, as learning demands, and find activities that suggest or require using the word wall. Ask students to come up with ways to use the word wall.

You also build a rich vocabulary through

- lots of reading
- intentional and thoughtful conversations
- repeated experiences of hearing varied and interesting words
- multiple exposures to a word in various contexts over time

Hodgepodge

Surprise students by spreading the contents of one or more purses, pockets, or drawers on a tabletop. Assign a vocabulary word to each student. Direct the students to scan the objects on the table to find one that can be associated in some way with their word. The challenge is to use the name of the object and the word sensibly in a sentence.

Example:

*The word **ostentatious** might be paired with a penny. The sentence might be, "A penny is the least **ostentatious** of all American coins."*

Picture That!

Keep a collection of pictures from magazines or newspapers. Give each student a picture along with one of the vocabulary words from the week's list. The student's job is to find at least one way to connect the word to that picture that shows his or her understanding of the meaning and present an explanation to the class.

Words on the Move

As often as possible, get students MOVING to show the meaning of the word they are trying to learn. Watch for words to which you can MOVE all or part of your body (*e.g., meander, gambol, cease, undulate, jubilation, retreat, stalk, gyrate, plod, cadence, pivot*).

Crazy Couplets

Divide students into groups of two or three, assigning a word to each group. Each group must write at least two different couplets that use the word in context and give a hint about the meaning of the word.

Examples:
*The wolf was **incognito** because he understood*
A disguise would make it easy to snatch Red Riding Hood.

After the president's unpopular veto,
*He had to visit Congress **incognito**.*

Cartoon Capers

Let students create cartoons that serve as mnemonic devices for remembering words. Share and post these cartoons. This strategy combines four brain-smart strategies that help with retention: humor, visual representation, emotion, and mnemonics. *(Save copies of the cartoons to use in teaching these words to other classes.)*

It's a serious
BLUNDER
to leave a cat alone
with a blender!

Beach Ball Banter

All year long, make a concerted effort to keep all the words from your vocabulary lists alive. It is like keeping a beach ball in the air at the seashore and trying not to let it touch the ground. Using vocabulary words never stops! In fact, use a REAL beach ball to play a game to remember and use such words. Toss a beach ball into the air. Each person who catches it must toss it on. When you say STOP! the student holding the beach ball must quickly choose one of the week's words from the wall and use it correctly in a statement or question. The game resumes and continues for a few minutes. *(You might make a rule that a word cannot be used twice during one game.)*

Memory Movers

Small groups work together to create sentences, riddles, jokes, or phrases that contain both the assigned vocabulary word and a mnemonic (memory mover) to help the brain remember the meaning of the vocabulary word.

Example:
Our parrot imitates every fancy melody he hears.
*It's uncanny that a parrot is so clever at **parody**!*

Words that Woo

Assign two vocabulary words to a small group. The group is to use the words in a billboard advertisement. The purpose is to woo the billboard viewer to try a product, come to an event, support a cause, or visit a place of business. The assigned words, in some form, must appear in print as part of the ad, along with any illustrations to support the message.

Draw It!

Drawing a picture can help anyone remember a new word. For instance, ask students to draw

- an **abridged** bridge
- a **petulant** pet
- an **embellished** belly

a **reclusive** rat

That's a Laugh!

Use humor when you present or explain a word to students. Then, once they know a word's meaning, set them loose to figure out a way to use humor to teach it to someone else. Examples:

- **Husbandry** has nothing to do with studying about how to get a husband, unless you want to be a good farmer's wife!
- **Irony** is not necessarily about ironing, but it would be ironic to give a steam iron to someone who has no electricity.
- **Acute** appendicitis is not the opposite of an ugly appendicitis. Ugly or cute, it's a severe, sharp pain!

Alarming Words!

Plant two or three hidden alarm clocks in the room; set them to go off at different moments during the class period. When an alarm sounds, dip your hand into the pot or box of names that you keep on your desk. The student whose name you draw finds the alarm, turns it off, and brings it to your desk, where it's traded for a (secret) vocabulary word. The student's job is to silently demonstrate or act out the meaning of the word.

Tête-à-têtes

Give pairs of students a few new words. BEFORE they learn the meanings, ask them to put their heads together to write sentences or questions using the words—just for fun. This will whet their interest in learning the actual meanings.

Student examples of sentences written without knowing the bold words:

- *Dr. **Verdant** prescribed **scruples** for the patient's fever.*
- *Don't **cornice** me with questions while I'm dancing the **macabre**!*
- *Could a **hovel** unbuckle that **debacle**?*
- *Jade's friends thought it was a **bellicose** idea to get her navel pierced.*
- *We ordered some canned chicken from the **chicanery**.*

Note to the Teacher:
ALWAYS take part in the activity so that you can seamlessly reinforce understandings and make connections as needed without stopping the pace and progress of the activity.

Show Off!

Show off any word that can possibly be demonstrated! **Do, act out, or show** any process, action, attitude, or concept that is named by one word! *Examples:*

disdain	appease	negligent	solemn	deplete
remorse	parallel	elusive	mitigate	pretentious
brevity	deter	retract	levity	peril
truculent	brawn	evaluate	pensive	synchrony
piety	juxtapose	extol	verbose	lachrymose

So What?

Help students deepen their understanding of words and the concepts related to or expressed by them by giving each student a word and asking him or her to build a list of one or more of the following about the word or the idea named by the word:

- *causes, effect, implications, consequences*
- *situations in which the student has seen or heard the word*
- *people (or places) that might be associated with it*
  (See the graphic organizer, *Digging Deeper*, on page 25.)

APPALLED

Let's Face It!

Draw faces to show the meaning or consequences of a word.
Example: *Draw a face to show the meaning of the word* **appalled.**

Keep the Tune. Change the Lyrics.

Set some words to music, and fix word meanings in the brain for a long time! Let students work in groups, each selecting a few of the week's words. Give them some time to write new lyrics to such familiar tunes as "Yankee Doodle," "Row, Row, Row Your Boat," "Old MacDonald," " The ABC Song," or "Happy Birthday." Or, groups can choose their own favorite melody. The song must include the vocabulary words, used in a way to demonstrate their meaning. Then, have each group sing their new songs to the class!

Confused

Students can clarify their understanding of words that are easily confused (such as *accept* and *except, flaunt* and *flout, loath* and *loathe, libel* and *slander, wax* and *wane*) by creating short sentences and questions.

Examples:

- *Laura has seen every "Spiderman" movie 20 times. Does she have a* **mania** *or a* **phobia?**
- *We predict she'll do the same with the next movie to be released. Is this a* **diagnosis** *or a* **prognosis?**
- *Her enthusiasm for "Spiderman" is spreading throughout her whole family. Is it* **contagious** *or* **infectious?**

24 English Language Arts: Tips for Teachers

Copyright © 2015 World Book, Inc./
Incentive Publications, Chicago, IL

Digging Deeper

Explore the deeper meanings of a word and the idea, feeling, situation, or concept it names.

The word _____

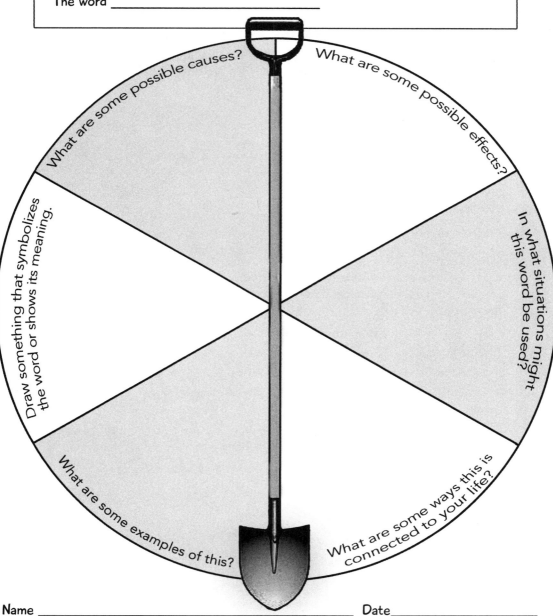

What are some possible causes?

What are some possible effects?

Draw something that symbolizes the word or shows its meaning.

In what situations might this word be used?

What are some examples of this?

What are some ways this is connected to your life?

Name _____ Date_____

Reminders for Teachers:

- Vocabulary is an essential component for student reading success and proficiency in writing. Beyond school, a rich vocabulary offers many benefits in the real world.

- Sound teaching strategies make a difference in whether words are forgotten or remembered.

- Presentation is everything. When you introduce new words, think of this as opening a box of chocolates, each with its own combination of ingredients. DO something that draws students to the word. (See the *Unforgettable!* list.) Clarify the meaning, examine the structure, and let students make fun, relevant, or surprising connections.

- Dig into the imaginary box of "word chocolates" every day, asking questions or conducting activities that require use of the words in all kinds of ways.

Matching Is for Socks!

Tips for Assessing Vocabulary Learning

Leave the matching for socks! Use better alternatives!

✓ Create assessment items that are unexpected in form and content. Think of inviting, amusing, and unusual ways to discern what has been learned. (See the examples on the next page.)

✓ Alter the evaluation process often and without notice.

✓ Test vocabulary in the same way that you teach vocabulary. Use the techniques from this chapter for assessment. (See the next page for more ideas.)

✓ Include analogies that can be completed only when word meanings are fully understood.

✓ Infuse reasoning skills into test items. Require a show of understanding or an application of the word, not just a rote memory of definitions.

✓ Evaluate knowledge through oral questions or directions to draw, apply, or demonstrate meanings.

Don't merely…
- match words from a list to their definitions.
- use a word from a list to fill the blank in a sentence.
- write a synonym for each word.
- write the definition of each word.

Examples of assessment items that can be answered on paper:

✓ What is something you would choose to *extol?*

✓ How would you *mitigate* the pain of a sunburn?

✓ An eighth-grade girl's diary is missing. Who might be *culpable?*

✓ Which are not examples of *ebullience?*
  a. Your dog rushes to meet you at the door, barking joyously.
  b. You accidentally drop your keys in the river and they sink.
  c. You are dreading the science test because you didn't study.

✓ Name a behavior that your parents would like you to *inhibit.*

✓ The math teacher tells the class to be ready for a quiz at any moment. Is the quiz *eminent* or *imminent?*

✓ Circle the word that is not used correctly. Write the word that should be in its place.
  We barely evacuated the hotel before smoke choked the hallways and flames incarcerated the entire party room.

✓ Which two words from the list are the best choices for describing a person who is easily irritated or whiny?

✓ Finish this rhyme to show you know the meaning of *clandestine.*
  When _____ ,
  I labeled that behavior as clandestine.

✓ How would you *cajole* someone into doing your chores?

✓ Draw something that would *oscillate.*

✓ Write a question you would ask a *gourmand.*

✓ When was the last time you were *obstreperous?*

✓ Name something you possess in *negligible* amounts.

✓ What could be a cause of *apathy?*

✓ Describe a *quandary* that might involve your laundry.

✓ Should you swim where there is a *dearth* of stinging jellyfish?

✓ What is a logical thing to do when you encounter a *juggernaut?*
  a. pour something into it.   c. run from it.
  b. play it in an orchestra.   d. download it onto your smart phone.

✓ Where would you find a *dictum*?
  a. in your liver   d. in a piece of music
  b. on a bagel   e. under a fingernail
  c. in a speech   f. around a wrist

Chapter 2

Give Students Powerful Reading Strategies for Any Content

Practical Tips for Helping Students Before, During, and After Reading

by Dr. Sharon Faber

A Game Plan for Reading

Today's teachers have access to well-researched guidelines and standards about what students are expected to know and be able to do. But, such standards do not tell what to teach, how to teach it, or how to adapt it to different learners. So a game plan for effective literacy teaching in any content area **must** include an understanding of skills that readers need for comprehension of any material, a collection of strategies and tools to help students gain those skills, and the knowledge to choose and use the right mix of strategies for individual readers.

With today's rapid technology changes, reading skills have ventured into spaces and places unimagined just a few years ago. As you implement reading strategies, apply them to texts in multiple formats, including e-books, web articles, visual presentations, social media sites, and other material transmitted digitally. (See pages 8 through 11 for technology-connection ideas.)

Comprehension Skills Needed for Reading Any Content

PREDICTING—*making an intelligent guess using prior knowledge and/or experience*
Good readers are curious about what they will find when they read. Making a *prediction* before reading silently helps motivate students to discover something new as they read.

CLARIFYING—*knowing when there are problems with understanding and how to resolve those problems as they occur; using fix-up strategies*
Good readers use metacognition strategies (thinking about thinking) when they read. They *clarify* their purpose for reading before they read, monitor their understanding as they read, and check their understanding of what they have read after reading.

QUESTIONING—*asking questions to help construct meaning while reading*
Good readers ask *questions* of themselves, the author (virtually), and the text during all stages of reading. They often challenge what the author says when something does not make sense.

SUMMARIZING—*a synthesis of the important ideas in a text*
Good readers can identify or *summarize* the main ideas of a text, connect the main ideas, eliminate redundant or unnecessary information, and remember what they read.

Three Stages of Reading Instruction

The teacher must always plan three stages of reading instruction—before, during, and after reading the text.

Before students read, the teacher needs to:
- Build background knowledge and purpose for the lesson.
- Pre-teach important or new concepts or vocabulary.
- Relate new information to previously learned information.
- Interpret visuals (charts, graphics, maps, pictures, etc.) and the captions.
- Review the questions students are to answer as and after they read.
- Ask students to predict what they might learn when they read.

While students read, the teacher needs to:
- Pair students to read to each other, in unison, or silently. Then they take turns retelling the information in their own words. Partners should be told to elaborate or add any missing content.
- Read aloud and have students follow along. At designated words or phrases, pause and ask the students to fill in the missing words.
- Call on a student to read, then have that student call on the next person. Students have the right to pass and then call on another person.
- Instruct students to keep learning logs or journals so they can think about what they are understanding and not understanding as they read (metacognition).
- Provide them with ways to map chapters, create webs, and analyze semantic features.
- Use socializing approaches—cooperative learning, peer editing, paired reading, writing a commercial, producing a radio show, debate, etc.
- Activate and use prior student knowledge and reflect on new understanding.
- Teach fix-up strategies—predict, clarify, reread the text, read on, question, and summarize.
- Pause during in-class reading to have students predict.

After students read, the teacher needs to:
- Discuss the content and synthesize the concepts that were learned.
- Review the significant or new terms or vocabulary.
- Extend the lesson through writing, projects (e.g., creating a summarizing videocast, comic strip, or timeline), dramatization, student-created games, role-playing of characters, or other type of enrichment activity.
- After reading informational texts, ask these five questions:
  1. *What are the answers to our questions about what we were reading?*
  2. *For which questions (if any) did we not find the answers?*
  3. *What else did you learn that we didn't think about?*
  4. *What is the most surprising or interesting thing we read or learned?*
  5. *What do we know now that we didn't know before?*

Instructional Strategies Before Reading

1. Book, Chapter, or Section Walk

Purpose: To create interest, assess or activate prior knowledge; to encourage personal connection to the text; to require active participation with the text; to expose students to critical text features; to develop purpose for reading; and to develop key concepts, vocabulary, and a general idea of the text before reading.

Process:

- Before students read, preview the parts of a book, story, article, chapter, or section by systematically examining the various visual and text features.
- Show cover, opening page, and first paragraph or beginning section and ask students to make predictions regarding content.
- Quickly walk through the text, pointing out key information and new vocabulary.
- Point out the text features that characterize the text and discuss why they are suited to the purpose of the text—title, table of contents, introduction, summary, main headings, boldface or italics, first and last paragraphs, graphics (such as charts, pictures, diagrams, or graphs), source, date, author, glossary, and sidebars.
- Use key vocabulary from the reading selection as you do the walk.
- As you go along, have students predict what the things you are pointing out will provide them. You may choose to record predictions.
- Return to predictions after reading.

2. List-Group-Label   Adapted from: Taba, H. (1967)

Purpose: To create interest and motivation to read, clarify misconceptions, activate prior knowledge, and develop clearer understandings about concepts.

Process:

- Select a key topic, concept, or idea.
- Instruct students to individually brainstorm words, phrases, names, or ideas related to the topic.
- Place students in pairs or trios and instruct them to combine their lists of words into groups or categories and give each category a label or descriptive term.
- Ask pairs or trios to share their lists and labels with the class and give reasons for their choices. There are no wrong answers if the groups and labels can be justified.
- Using their group lists, ask students to develop a list of questions they want answered or ideas they want clarified during the reading of the text.
- Tell students to read the text to see if their groups and labels were correct or if they would like to modify their work after reading the text.

3. Anticipation Guides Adapted from: Tierney, R. J., Readence, J. E., & Dishner, E. K. (1995)

Purpose: To activate prior knowledge; to create curiosity about the selection; to encourage personal and real-world connections to the text; to require active participation with the text; and to motivate students to read.

Process:

List five to seven statements that:

- address the major topics, themes, concepts, or issues of the text;
- present important generalizations;
- are worth discussing and will encourage thinking and debate;
- do not have clear-cut or yes-or-no answers; and
- are experience-based, if possible.
  Note: Anticipation guides are useful for all three stages of reading.
  See a template for an anticipation guide on page 36.

Before reading:

- Give students the statements. Have them mark A (agree) or D (disagree) on their papers and share answers with a partner.
- Ask for a show of hands as to whether they agree or disagree with each statement.
- Ask students to give reasons for their opinions.
- Do not correct answers.

During reading:

- Instruct students to take notes on the topics or issues.
- Ask students to document the location (page, column, paragraph, line) of confirming or conflicting information.
- Remind students to read critically and with a purpose.
- Encourage students to examine the issues with an open mind or from a fresh point of view.

After reading:

- Review original responses. See if students feel the same or if they have changed their thinking.
- Use the following questions to guide discussion:
  1. *What information did you learn that you did not "anticipate" before you read?*
  2. *What have you learned by reading this selection?*
  3. *What was the most interesting, surprising, or unusual information you learned?*
  4. *What other questions do you still have about the topic or text?*
  5. *Do you trust the expertise and credentials of the author? Why?*

Instructional Strategies During Reading

1. Sorts

Purpose: To actively manipulate content and vocabulary using the mind-body connection; to develop spelling, vocabulary, and comprehension skills; to develop clearer understandings about concepts.

Process:

- Write the terms, concepts, ideas, or problems on cards or strips of paper.
- Place the cards or paper strips in resealable plastic bags or envelopes.
- Have students work in pairs or alone to match or sort the terms.
- Assign a category for sorting: word definition, antonym or synonym, cause/effect, questions/answers, alphabetical, sequential, chronological, meaning, form, or function.

2. Reciprocal Teaching Adapted from: Palincsar, A. S., & Brown, A. L. (1985)

Purpose: To help students make sense of the text; to focus and monitor reading comprehension; to develop skills in predicting, questioning, clarifying, and summarizing; to make connections with text during the reading.

Process:

- The teacher models each of the four comprehension skills—**predict, question, clarify,** and **summarize**—by using a short passage of text as an example before students begin the process:
    1. *Predict* what you think will happen next.
    2. Generate *questions* you have about the text or questions someone might ask you about the text.
    3. Stop and attempt to *clarify* words, ideas, concepts, and sentences in the text by talking about what is your best guess about these elements.
    4. *Summarize* what you think are the most important ideas the author would want you to take away from the reading.
- Give students a four-column chart listing the four skills they will use in their reading: predict, question, clarify, and summarize.
- Put students in groups of four and assign each student a role: summarizer, questioner, clarifier, and predictor. Divide the reading into four sections and switch roles so that each student will have a chance to perform in all four roles.
- Students assume their roles and read a few paragraphs of the selection, taking notes on key information.
- When they stop at a given point, the summarizer will give the major points; the questioner will ask questions about unclear parts, puzzling information, or new words; the clarifier will address the confusing parts and try to answer the questions; and the predictor will guess what will happen next or what will be learned as they read.

3. Say Something

Purpose: To make connections with the text during reading; to help students make sense of the text and enhance comprehension; and to increase skills in questioning, predicting, summarizing, and clarifying.

Process:
- Select text to be read and assign students to pairs.
- Designate a stopping point in the selection, or an amount of time.
- Have students read to the stopping point, at which time each one must "say something" about the text to the partner.
- Students can retell facts they have learned, question information, summarize information, clarify confusing information, point out a detail that supports a main idea, or make a connection to some real-world event, using such stems as:

Ask a **question** of the text:
(who, what, when, where, why, how)
What does _____ mean?
Who is _____ ?

Connect a past experience to the text:
I once *(saw, heard, felt, did, read)* something like this text.

Make a **prediction** (intelligent guess) about the text:
I think _____ will happen.

Make a free **comment** about the text:
I (like, don't like) this story because _____ .

Make an **inference** (educated guess) from the text:
The text says _____ .
I say _____ .
So _____ .

Clarify (make clear) something in the text by paraphrasing or elaborating:
Now I understand _____; it means _____ .
_____ makes sense now; it is _____ .

- Allow pairs to choose the next stopping point in the text. If the text has subheadings, these make good stopping points. Students repeat the "say something" process until they have finished reading the text.

Instructional Strategies After Reading

1. QAR: Question-Answer Relationships Adapted from: Raphael, T. 1982 and 1986

Purpose: To encourage personal connection to the text, require active reading of the text, learn how to find answers based on type of question.

Process:

- Teach the four types of Question-Answer Relationships. The first two types of questions are literal and in the text. The last two are inferential and require some prior knowledge.

- Have students practice what kind of question they are answering.

  Right There: The answer is in a single sentence, and the words in the question are in the text. There is usually only one correct answer, and it is one word or short phrase. *Example:* Who was the 16th president of the United States? Text: The 16th president of the United States was . . .

  Think and Search: The answer is in the text but requires looking in several sentences or paragraphs to find the answer. *Example:* Compare the function of roots to the function of stems in a plant. Text location:

  Author and You: The answer is not in the text, but the text must be read to answer the question. Information the author gives is combined with prior knowledge. *Example:* Today we read about life during the 1700's. How does life today differ from life then?

  On my own: The answer is not in the text, and it is based on personal belief and prior knowledge. *Example:* Now that we have studied nutrition, what do you think are the most important things the human body needs in order to stay healthy? (Although the answer is not in the text, students can find information in the text that supports or complements their beliefs and prior knowledge.)

2. ABC Brainstorming Review

Purpose: To check background knowledge; to note key elements or information; or to create a summary or review.

Process:

- Students list letters of the alphabet down a sheet of paper (or you provide them with a sheet with the alphabet boxes).

- Students fill in key words or phrases from the text that begin with each letter (in no particular order).

- Begin individually; then allow students to pair up.

- Have students share answers with the class, write a summary paragraph that includes what they think are the major points, or create a graphic organizer of what they have learned.

3. Somebody Wanted But So (SWBS)

Purpose: To reduce text to main ideas, enabling students to distinguish between important and unimportant information in the text. Selecting only the most important information is the difficult part of summarizing for students, because they believe everything written in the text must be important!

Process:

- Teach students the categories of SWBS technique.
- Model examples. (Start with a story everyone knows. See below.)
- Some texts can involve more than one SWBS statement, often because there are subplots, multiple important events, or more than one critical person.
- SWBS can be used to write one summary statement by connecting the parts with "and" or "then" or "next."

Somebody....... Person, characters, country (*"Three Little Pigs"*)

Wanted .... Motivation: The gist of the issue; what somebody is trying to accomplish, achieve, or acquire.

(They wanted to build strong houses to keep them safe from the wolf.)

But .... The problem: What is the obstacle to success, the conflict or opposition?

(The wolf was powerful enough to blow down the house made of straw and the house made of sticks.)

So.................... How the problem is solved

(So the first two pigs ran to the house of the third pig, who had built a house of bricks.)

Then................ Resolution: the ending or outcome

(Then the wolf huffed and puffed, but could not blow down the brick house. When the wolf tried to climb down the chimney, the pigs had a pot of boiling water waiting to catch him.)

One-sentence summary:

_____ wanted _____ (somebody) but _____ so

then _____ .

Reproduce this page at 120% for 8½ x 11 size.

Anticipate and Reflect

Use this guide to prepare for and later review your reading assignment.

• **Before you read,** circle A or D to show whether you agree or disagree with each statement.

• **While you read,** record page number(s) to show where you found answers or information on each statement.

• **After you read,** reflect on your original choice: Would you change your marking (A or D)? What new information did you learn?

my reflections!

Statement	Agree or Disagree	Page(s)	Reflection
	A / D		
	A / D		
	A / D		
	A / D		
	A / D		
	A / D		
	A / D		

Name _____   Date_____

Guidelines for Selecting Reading Strategies

Select strategies that:

1 you can explicitly teach through the context of your content.

2 work well with your content.

3 students can use over and over with supported and structured practice.

4 you can model and explain using your content.

> The challenge for the teacher of any content area is to determine what strategies will help students acquire the content knowledge while managing the wide range of differences in reading achievement.

Guidelines for Effectively Teaching Reading Strategies

1 Provide instruction before, during, and after reading the text.

2 Promote thinking and elaboration by asking questions, encouraging student questions and discussion, and using a variety of scaffolding techniques (e.g., relating text to previous knowledge, using a graphic organizer, or pausing to reflect and review) for reading new and difficult text.

3 Explain, model, and guide practice until students apply strategies independently, flexibly, and in combination.

4 Provide explicit instruction for each strategy.

5 Prepare for instruction by anticipating specific problems that students will encounter in your content (such as need for prior knowledge, vocabulary, sentence structure, literary techniques, or fluency).

6 Use ongoing monitoring to adjust instruction, correct misconceptions, and measure progress.

Questions Good Readers Ask Themselves

Before Reading

- What do I need to know before I read this material?

- What do I already know about this topic?

- How is the text organized to help me understand what I read?

- What is the reason I am reading this material?

- What is the author's reason for writing this material?

During Reading

- How does this information connect to what I already know?

- How does what I am reading compare to what I thought I knew?

- Does what I am reading make sense? If it does not, what is it that I don't understand?

- Do I need to mark important words or ideas? Are there words and ideas that I don't know?

- What are the key points made or messages communicated?

- What details give support to or convince readers of the main points?

- What mental pictures do I see?

- Who or what is the reading about?

- When and where does the information take place?

- How and why do the events happen?

- Is there a specific problem that is solved? How is it solved?

After Reading

- Did I find the answers to the questions I needed to answer?

- Did I learn what I wanted to learn?

- Were there other questions that I found or answers I didn't find?

- What do I know now that I didn't know before?

- What new terms, concepts, or vocabulary did I learn?

- How has this text affected me, or what effect may it have on other readers?

- How can I restate the main points in my own words?

- How can I apply what I just read to my schoolwork and my life?

Characteristics of Struggling and Strong Readers

Before Reading

Struggling	Strong
Reluctant to read or resists reading tasks	Confidently approaches reading tasks
Has limited background knowledge—no idea where to begin	Activates prior knowledge on the subject before reading—thinks about the content and what he or she already knows
Rarely has or can remember background knowledge relating to the new learning	Connects background knowledge to the new learning
Reads without a clear purpose	Knows the purpose for reading
Reads without considering how to approach the material	Makes predictions and chooses appropriate strategies to understand the reading
Sets minimal goals or no goals for understanding the text	Sets relevant, attainable goals based on the purpose for reading

Effective reading helps students make connections between what they already know and the new information being presented. Teachers must teach students how to use reading as a tool for thinking and learning in all subjects, using instructional approaches that reflect differences in text features among the subject areas.

During Reading

Struggling	Strong
Has a limited attention span	Focuses complete attention on reading
Needs guidance for reading tasks	Is able to read independently
Has a limited vocabulary	Possesses an extensive vocabulary
Rarely applies word attack skills	Uses a variety of decoding or word attack skills
Reads word by word, lacks fluency	Reads fluently
Does not monitor comprehension • does not recognize text structures • reads everything at the same rate, often very slowly • reads to get it done • gives up when reading is difficult or uninteresting • does not integrate information, understands only pieces • does not ask relevant questions • rarely creates mental images while reading • does not realize he or she does not understand the content or know how to correct lack of understanding • does not recognize important vocabulary • does not use context clues	Monitors comprehension • uses text structure to assist with comprehension • adjusts reading rate according to purpose • reads to learn; anticipates and predicts meaning • perseveres through unfamiliar passages • integrates new information by searching for main ideas and inferring • raises relevant questions • creates visual and sensory images from the text—"movie in the head" • knows when he or she does not understand content and uses fix-up strategies (reread, read aloud, etc.) • strives to understand new terms • uses context clues
Uses a limited number of fix-up strategies	Is flexible according to the reading task

"That the brain learns to read at all attests to its remarkable ability to sift through seemingly confusing input and establish patterns and systems. For a few children, this process comes naturally; most have to be taught."

David Sousa, 2011

After Reading

Struggling	Strong
Forgets or confuses information	Reflects on what he or she reads and adds new information to knowledge base
Looks only for "the answer" and gives verbatim responses	Summarizes major ideas and recalls supporting details, makes inferences, draws conclusions, paraphrases
Does not read outside of school	Seeks additional information from outside sources
Feels success is unattainable, sees it as a result of luck	Feels success is a result of effort
Relies on the teacher for information	Can independently obtain information
Expresses negative feelings about reading	Expresses opinions about or pleasure in selections read
Avoids reading at all costs	Chooses to read for the sheer joy of it

References

Palincsar, A. S., & Brown, A. L. (1985). Reciprocal teaching: Activities to promote "reading with your mind." In T. L. Harris & E. J. Cooper (Eds.), *Reading, thinking and concept development: Strategies for the classroom*. New York: College Board.

Raphael, T. (1982). *Improving question-answering performance through instruction*. Reading Education Report No. 32. Champaign, IL: University of Illinois at Urbana-Champaign.

Raphael, T. E. (1986). Teaching question answer relationships, revisited. In *The Reading Teacher* 39 (6): 516-522.

Sousa, D. (2011). *How the brain learns* (4th ed.). Thousand Oaks, CA: Corwin Press.

Taba, H. (1967). *Teachers' handbook for elementary social studies*. Reading, MA: Addison-Wesley.

Tierney, R. J., Readence, J. E., & Dishner, E. K. (1995). *Reading strategies and practices*. Boston: Allyn & Bacon.

Chapter 3

Turn Students Into Text Detectives

*Practical Tips to Help Teachers Foster Text Analysis
and Critical Thinking Skills*

by Marjorie Frank

Read Deeply! Examine Closely!

Text analysis is a method of approaching any text—literary or informational—with a natural curiosity that leads readers to seek to understand written selections and connect them to other texts or presentations and to their world. When students set out to analyze texts, they literally become detectives—following clues, gathering evidence, making educated guesses, interpreting information, and reaching informed conclusions. To grow in the skills of text analysis, students examine a work to:

- determine main ideas, claims, and themes (explicit and implicit)
- notice and describe the development of key ideas, claims, and themes
- identify evidence in the text that support writers' claims or ideas
- find meaning and relevance in a text
- examine the text structure and the purpose it serves
- interpret the language used in the text
- examine and analyze an author's style, viewpoint, bias, and tone
- recognize how writers use language to engage readers and convey messages
- make reasoned evaluations about the effects and effectiveness of the author's craft, the effectiveness and validity of the ideas, and how well the author accomplished his or her purpose

In the lives of students today, many "texts" they encounter and "read" are not printed on a page. Thanks to electronic devices, literally thousands of texts are available to teachers and students for use as learning tools. Consciously use the terms "text" and "read" in the broader sense—to refer to any presentation of a literary or informational work. The same skills of analysis used for written texts can and should be applied to works students watch; listen to; hear; or experience from live performances, videos, apps, Internet sources, movies, songs, or from any number of digital platforms. See that students have multiple experiences with varied kinds of "reading" experiences and opportunities for response available through the technology in their environments. (See pages 8 through 11 for technology-connection ideas.)

Literary Text Analysis Skills Checklist

Understand What Is Said

_____ Find, explain, and interpret main points and key arguments (literal and implied).

_____ Paraphrase or summarize the work.

_____ Explain meanings of words and phrases in context.

_____ Identify the writer's purpose for the selection.

_____ Recognize from whose point of view the piece is created and how this matters.

_____ Conjecture how the selection might be written from a different point of view.

Analyze and Explain the Meanings

_____ Draw reasoned conclusions about the meanings of the selection.

_____ Present ample evidence and details from the text to support your conclusions.

_____ Use evidence from the text to make predictions, form inferences, and note implications.

_____ Explain how the author's stylistic choices contribute to the meaning.

_____ Identify the underlying themes and ideas of the selection (e.g., search for love, revenge, survival, quest for identity, redemption, forgiveness, time, death, alienation, sense of belonging, etc.).

Judge the Effectiveness

_____ Make reasoned judgments about the effectiveness of the selection in accomplishing its purpose or conveying the intended message.

_____ Use specific, relevant evidence from the text to support your judgments.

_____ Evaluate the effectiveness of specific components of the author's techniques and choices.

_____ Compare two or more texts with similar messages or purposes; use evidence from the texts to evaluate their effectiveness at communicating the messages or purposes.

Make Meaningful Connections

_____ Explore and explain how the message, theme, or meaning relates to real life experiences, events, issues, or situations.

_____ Discuss possibilities for transferring messages, lessons, or meanings from the selection to other contexts, disciplines, people, events, issues, places, or times.

Good Questions to Ask about Literature

After answering any question below, follow up with students by asking, "How do you know?"
Also, listen and look for their use of evidence from the text to support their answers.

- What is the author trying to say? What big ideas or issues are addressed?

- What is explicit? What is implicit?

- What is the theme (or main message)? How is it developed?

- How does the author use language to accomplish the purpose or convey the message?

- What techniques of craft does the author use? How do they contribute to the meaning?

- Who is telling the story? How can you tell? What is his or her perspective?

- What is the primary effect of the author's description of _____?

- What purpose is served by the writer's allusion to _____ ?

- What does this phrase or sentence: (_____) tell about the character?

- What is the writer's attitude? How can you tell? How does this affect the reader?

- What symbolism is used? How does it contribute to the meaning?

- How would you interpret this line (or phrase, sentence, paragraph, section)?

- What does _____ (name a literary device) contribute to the piece?

- What attitudes, stereotypes, or prejudices are evident from the writing? How can you tell?

- How does the setting help to create a mood?

- What is the author's style? What leads you to define the style this way?

- How does the style affect the reader or the message?

- What do these words or phrases: (_____) contribute to the meaning (or theme, mood, or tone)?

- What is the tone? What effect does it have on the message?

- How would you paraphrase these lines: (_____) ?

- The author repeatedly uses metaphorical language. What effect does that have?

- How does the writer use imagery (or any device) to reveal her attitude about _____ ?

- What techniques does the writer use to build the conflict in the selection?

- How would you describe the writer's voice? What techniques contribute to that voice?

- The writer draws the conclusion that _____ . What evidence is given to support this conclusion? Is it enough?

- Does the writer's style successfully contribute to the development of the plot?

- What techniques in the presentation distract from the message or story?

- What other works address the same message or theme? How do the works compare?

Literary Text Analysis

Name _____ Date _____

Section Title _____

Author _____ Source _____

Why did you choose this selection?	What was the theme or main message?	What techniques did the author use to communicate the theme or main message?

Describe the structure of the selection.

How did the structure affect the theme or main ideas?

What part of the story or poem is most powerful, and why?

Brief passage that communicates the theme or central idea:

Student Scoring Guide for Literary Text Analysis

Use this guide to reflect on your analysis of any literary text.

Score	Understanding — *Identify purpose and glean major themes and messages; provide reasoned, supported conclusions*	Analyzing — *Recognize and analyze how the author conveys the message*	Evaluating — *Evaluate the author's message and effectiveness and connect meanings to broader contexts*
5	• I have shown understanding of the work and the author's purpose, theme, or main message. • I have drawn reasoned conclusions about the meaning and significance, and supported them thoroughly with evidence from the text. • I can summarize the central ideas of the text.	• I present an insightful analysis of the author's use of literary elements and devices, and of the author's stylistic choices (diction, syntax, rhetoric). • I have thoroughly examined and explained how these choices by the author affected the message and the reader.	• I show carefully reasoned judgments about how well the author accomplished the purpose and about how effectively writing techniques were used. • I have specific evidence to support my evaluations. • I have done a thorough job of connecting this to my other texts and real life experiences.
3	• My response shows some understanding of the work and the author's purpose, theme, or main message. • I have drawn a few conclusions about the meaning, with limited evidence. • I can summarize a few of the central ideas of the text.	• My analysis of the author's ideas and techniques is limited. • I have given simple explanations as to how the author's craft and ideas affected the meaning and message.	• My response contains some judgments about the author's effectiveness. • I have some evidence from the text to support my judgments. • I have connected the text to other texts or real-life situations.
1	• My response shows no understanding (or a misunderstanding) of the author's message, theme, and purpose. • I have drawn no conclusions about the meaning. • I am not able to provide a clear summary of the central ideas.	• I have identified few or no elements or techniques used by the author; I have not explained how the author's craft affected the meaning.	• My response shows no judgments about the author's technique or message, or I have given no evidence to support my opinion. • I have not related this selection to my life or other experiences.

Note: A score of 4 may be given where analytical work falls between a score of 3 and 5; or a score of 2 may be given where analytical work falls between a score of 1 and 3.

Informational Text Analysis Skills Checklist

Understand What Is Said

___ Find, explain, and interpret central ideas or arguments (and counterarguments).

___ Describe the development of an idea or claim throughout the text.

___ Explain meanings of words and phrases (including figurative language) in context.

___ Identify the author's purpose for the selection.

___ Recognize the point of view of the selection and how this matters.

___ Provide a summary of the central ideas of the text.

Recognize and Evaluate How It Is Said

___ Identify specific devices and techniques the author uses to accomplish a purpose or convey a message, attitude, tone, or effect, and describe how they are used.

___ Describe an author's style and the factors that contribute to it.

___ Explain how the author's stylistic choices contribute to the meaning and purpose.

___ Describe an author's voice, explain how it is manifested, and identify its effects on the meaning or on the reader.

___ Describe the structure of a selection and recognize its effects on the meaning.

Analyze and Explain the Meanings

___ Draw reasoned conclusions about the meanings of the selection.

___ Present ample evidence and details from the text to support your conclusions.

___ Use evidence from the text to make inferences and predictions.

___ Identify the underlying themes, ideas, or claims of the selection; identify and interpret implicit messages.

Judge the Effectiveness

___ Make reasoned judgments about the effectiveness of the selection in accomplishing its purpose or conveying a message.

___ Use specific, relevant evidence from the text to support your judgments.

___ Identify arguments in a text (the evidence presented, the reasoning behind them) and the effectiveness of the author in making the argument.

___ Evaluate the effectiveness of specific components of the author's craft.

___ Give reasoned evaluations (with supporting details) as to the validity of the conclusions reached by the writer.

Make Meaningful Connections

___ Explore and explain how the meaning, conclusions, or facts relate to real life experiences, events, issues, or situations.

___ Discuss possibilities for transferring messages, information, lessons, or meanings from the selection to other contexts, disciplines, people, places, or times.

Good Questions to Ask about Informational Text

After answering any question below, follow up with students by asking, "How do you know?" Also, listen and look for the students' use of evidence from the text to support their answers.

- What is unique about this genre?
- What is explicit in this text? What is implicit?
- What are the central ideas or key claims?
- What details are most helpful in supporting the central ideas?
- What is the author's purpose? How can you tell?
- What did the writer do best?
- Whose viewpoint is reflected in this passage?
- How does the author hook and hold the reader?
- How does the writer use language to convey key ideas?
- What did you know before reading this work that is related to this topic or idea?
- What's new here? What did you learn from reading this?
- What supported some things you already knew?
- What in your reading offered a different message or information than you had received previously on the subject?
- Where have you seen this idea before?
- What puzzled you? Excited you? Interested you most? Surprised you? Confused you?
- What biases are evident in the writing? How can you tell?
- What is the writer's attitude toward _____ ? How can you tell?
- How does the structure of the work help you understand the meaning?
- What other structure might be used to communicate this same message or information? How would the different structure affect the message?
- Did the author give credible evidence sufficient to substantiate the claims?
- Does the author present opposing viewpoints? If so, how?
- How are emotional strategies (or logical strategies) used to promote an idea or message?
- How effectively does the writer convey the message or accomplish the purpose? What contributed to the effectiveness or ineffectiveness?
- How does this text connect to the real world?
- Compare two pieces on the same topic that have different structures. What are the benefits or drawbacks of each structure? Which piece argues the point or presents the information more effectively? Why?
- How might you transfer this message or idea to something else?
- So what? (What difference does this work make? What effect might this work have?)

Informational Text Analysis

Name _____ Date _____

Selection Title _____ Author _____

Reflect on each question or task before answering.

- What is the author's purpose?

- What was the author's attitude about the subject?

- What did you know about the topic before you read this?

- How did the structure of the selection affect the message?

- What new information did you learn?

- What techniques did the author use that made the selection effective or ineffective?

- Did this confirm or contradict anything you already knew?

- How well did the author accomplish the purpose?

Summarize the main message or idea.

Student Scoring Guide for Informational Text Analysis

Use this guide to reflect on your analysis of any informational text.

Score	**Understanding** *Identify purpose and glean major themes and messages; provide reasoned, supported conclusions*	**Analyzing** *Recognize and analyze how the author conveys the message*	**Evaluating** *Evaluate the author's message and effectiveness and connect meanings to broader contexts*
5	• My response shows a deep understanding of the work and its purpose, central ideas, or claims. • I have drawn reasoned conclusions about the meaning and significance, and supported them thoroughly with evidence from the text. • I can summarize the central ideas or claims and counterclaims of the text.	• I present an insightful analysis of the author's use of text structure, language, and writing style. • I have thoroughly examined and explained how these choices by the author affected the message and the reader.	• I show carefully reasoned judgments about how well the author accomplished the purpose and about how effectively writing techniques were used. • I use specific evidence to support evaluations. • I have connected this well to other texts, contexts, and real life experiences.
3	• My response shows some understanding of the work and the author's purpose, theme, or main message. • I have drawn a few conclusions about the meaning, with limited evidence. • I can summarize a few of the central ideas or claims and counterclaims of the text.	• My analysis of the author's ideas and techniques is limited. • I have given simple explanations as to how the author's craft and ideas affected the meaning and message.	• My response contains some judgments about the author's effectiveness. • I gave simple or limited evidence from the text to support my judgments. • I have made some connections to other texts, contexts, and real-life experiences.
1	• My response shows no understanding (or a misunderstanding) of the author's message, theme, and purpose. • I have drawn no conclusions about the meaning. • I cannot summarize the central ideas or claims and counterclaims of the text.	• I have identified few or no techniques used by the author; I have not explained how the author's craft affected the meaning.	• My response shows no judgments about the author's technique or message, or I have given no evidence to support my opinion. • I have not related this selection to texts, contexts, and real-life experiences.

Note: A score of 4 may be given where analytical work falls between a score of 3 and 5; or a score of 2 may be given where analytical work falls between a score of 1 and 3.

Chapter 4

Guide Writing from Beginning Blunderings to Polished Pieces

Practical Tips to Help Teachers Plan for Successful Writing Instruction

by Marjorie Frank

Teaching for Effective Writing

Below are some of the things that experience and research tells us about the best practices that lead to effective student writing:

- Model enthusiasm for writing. Show students that you take writing seriously.
- Write **with** students. Share with students examples of your own writing.
- Connect writing to reading—constantly! Provide many models of effective writing.
- Don't ask students to write cold (without some experience or discussion to help the ideas flow) on a prescribed topic.
- Let students write freely without stopping to correct grammar and mechanics.
- Address students' attitudes about writing. (Ask such questions as: *How do you feel when you're asked to write? What are your past experiences with writing?*)
- Give separate, explicit instruction on each stage of the writing process.
- Teach specific writing traits and techniques separately.
- Use **short** activities to teach and practice skills.
- **Write together** often (as a class, or in pairs, or small groups).
- Write about familiar real-world topics, questions, issues, and experiences.
- Write for a variety of audiences and purposes.
- Teach and write in many different genres and their structures (e.g., allegories, articles, arguments, characterizations, biographies, critiques, dialogues, dramas, editorials, letters, mysteries, myths, poems, reflections, satires, and tweets.)
- Set reasonable, attainable goals for revision. When revising, focus on strengths.
- Edit writing conventions (e.g., spelling, grammar, etc.) separately from other traits.
- Give more feedback (of good quality). Teach students to give feedback.
- Use a variety of technological tools (hardware and software) for all types of writing and for all stages of the writing process. (See pages 8 through 11 for technology-connection ideas for language arts learning.)

Writing Traits

Ideas – the message of the writing

Did you . . .

- know what you wanted to say and say it clearly?
- know your purpose and audience?
- choose ideas of appropriate complexity to the purpose and audience?
- choose ideas that fit together and did not wander?
- gather relevant information from credible sources to support a claim?
- include important, relevant, and specific examples and details to enrich and develop the theme or key message?
- keep the ideas focused on your main message or central ideas?
- include content that is unexpected or out of the ordinary?
- add details that "paint a picture" (**showing,** instead of telling, the reader)?

Organization – the way the piece is put together; the path that it follows

Did you . . .

- plan where your writing would go and keep a clear direction?
- choose a structure that would enhance the communication of your main ideas?
- write a strong beginning that grabs the reader's attention?
- write details in a logical sequence that leads from one idea to the next?
- include smooth transitions between points, ideas, or story parts?
- build the story or details up to a strong central idea, claim, or message?
- leave the reader with a memorable or convincing conclusion?

Words – the words and phrases you choose, and how you use them

Did you . . .

- choose colorful, precise words for the context?
- use active verbs?
- use words and phrases that create images and appeal to many senses?
- avoid overused words?
- choose words that effectively set the mood or tone you intended?
- choose words suited to the topic, purpose, and audience?
- avoid the overuse of adjectives and adverbs?
- use figurative language effectively?

Sentences – the clarity, sense, and fluency of your sentences; the way they sound alone and next to each other; the way they are structured

Did you . . .
- write sentences that flow smoothly?
- write sentences that appeal to the ear, free of awkward patterns?
- create sentences that sound interesting and have pleasing rhythms?
- vary sentence beginnings?
- vary sentence structures, styles, and length?
- write sentences that fit well together?

Voice – the way the writer's personality shows; the flavor and style of the writing

Did you . . .
- show **yourself** to the reader?
- talk directly to the reader?
- write in a way that shows you care about the message?
- write in a way that is authentic and distinctive?
- infuse the writing with honesty, passion, energy, and flair?
- help the reader get a feel for you as a real, live person?

Conventions – the way the rules of language are used

Did you . . .
- use correct capitalization and punctuation?
- form and indent paragraphs properly?
- present dialogue correctly?
- use accurate grammar?
- include accurate usage of language (e.g., verb tense, etc.)?
- spell as accurately as possible?

The Writing Process

Stage 1 — Romancing

Create a spark that will get ideas flowing. It might be an experience, a book, an unexpected question, a video clip, a sound or song, a discussion, a visitor, a trip, an art lesson, a piece of literature, a common feeling—any situation that stirs up impressions, emotions, questions, or opinions and brings to the surface the "imaginings" or ideas that are tucked away inside writers.

Choose high-interest sparks—ones that are fascinating and relevant to young writers.

Stage 2 — Collecting

Gather words, ideas, phrases, thoughts, facts, questions, details, or observations. This is the process of brainstorming and broadening the original idea—a creative stage that provides the raw material for writing.

Allow plenty of time for this and do it with your writers. Contribute your ideas, too.

Stage 3 — Organizing

Take a close look at each of the gathered ideas or pieces and think about what fits together. Group together words, phrases, examples, arguments, or details that support a main idea or claim. Decide which ideas belong in the same part of the piece.

This is often a hard stage. Do it together. Model good organization. Graphic organizers can help organize thoughts.

Stage 4 — Drafting

Make use of the inspiration (Stage 1), raw material (Stage 2), and organization (Stage 3), and **begin** writing. Start putting the piece together in lines, sentences, or paragraphs.

A blank page can be scary, but there will be less to fear if you've spent adequate time on stages 1–3. Allow plenty of time for this stage. Write without stopping to correct mechanics. Just get your thoughts on paper.

Stage 5 — Reviewing (by the author)

Get the writing out into the light. See how it looks and hear how it sounds.

The author asks: Does it make sense? Does it say what I meant? Is it clear and smooth? Are ideas in the right order? Is anything missing? Are any lines choppy? Are any words wrong or boring? Are main ideas well supported?

Stage 6 — Sharing for Response

Someone else responds to the writing. Responses should include praise, questions, and suggestions.

The author asks the responder: "What did I do well? What works? What did you like? What is missing? What is confusing? What didn't work?"

Model this stage frequently with the whole class or in smaller groups. Teach students the difference between compliments or suggestions that are helpful and those that give nothing of substance to the writer.

Stage 7 — Revising

Make changes. Take the reflections, add them to the responses and suggestions of others, and make choices about what needs to be revised and how.

Rework only a few areas at once. Tackling more may be overwhelming.

Stage 8 — Checking Conventions

Inspect the current draft for spelling, grammar, mechanical and structural errors, and weaknesses.

Writers may need help with this. Provide resources for students to use in checking grammar and spelling.

Stage 9 — Polishing

Write the final copy.

Writers may repeat some or all of stages 5–8 before they write the final copy.

Stage 10 — Presenting

Show off. Share. Publish. This stage dignifies the writing, gets it out into the open where it can be heard and admired, and gives writers a good reason for polishing.

*There are literally hundreds of ways to do this. Always give writers a chance to make the writing public **if** they choose, but never share a writer's work without permission.*

Tips for Helping Students Strengthen Their Writing

1 **The number one prerequisite for successful writing in the classroom** is a teacher who writes, who takes writing seriously, who loves the process, and who loves sharing his or her own and others' works. Be that person for your student writers!

2 **Read . . . read . . . read aloud to students.** This is an absolute **must** for effective teaching of writing. Make it a habit to share written pieces daily—all kinds of texts from all types of sources with many different styles, purposes, and genres. Choose short selections or short excerpts. Sometimes it might be only a unique sentence or catchy phrase. Share these with enthusiasm!

3 **Get into a mindset and habit of friendly analysis.** Point out examples of good writing everywhere you see it. Don't do this every single time a selection is read, but do it often. Stop and casually remark on (or ask students to notice) what the writer did well or how the writer accomplished a purpose or used a particular device, technique, or element. Find examples of good technique in students' writing. Teach students to do this! Turn them into device detectives—curious thinkers who are on the lookout for great examples of devices, techniques, and elements. Constantly be on the lookout for what the text says (explicitly and implicitly) and how the text says it. Dig deeply into the way writers communicate messages effectively. Pay attention to the voice, structure, organization, and word choice.

4 **Do more romancing.** Don't skimp on this first stage of the writing process. Take time to read, watch, share, experience, tell stories, question, eat, dance, dramatize, listen, watch, listen, and discuss. These are the processes that get ideas flowing and get writers ready to write. Most writers are not inspired by a "cold" writing assignment.

5 **Spend more time collecting.** Don't skimp on the second stage of the writing process. As writers do this step, they get more involved in the topic. If they collect plenty of ideas, words, phrases, facts, viewpoints, and background in this stage, the following stages will flow more smoothly because there will be plenty of raw material for organizing, drafting, and revising.

6 **Think short.** It is far easier to teach specific writing skills and techniques if students are writing short selections. Long selections have too many different elements to manage and, often, too many errors to fix.

7 **Use anonymous pieces.** When teaching specific traits or techniques for any stage of the writing process, use pieces written by writers other than the students. (This is less threatening for students, particularly when working on revision skills.) Collect samples from previous classes, other teachers, neighbors, your own children, or pieces you've written. Capture things from magazines, advertisements, websites, video clips, fliers, and newspapers. (Yes, many of these need revision!) Give students whole pieces or beginnings, endings, main ideas, theses, anecdotes, phrases, supportive details, or sentences to organize, analyze, or revise.

8 **Write together, with teacher direction.** The skills of writing are best taught when students work through the writing process together. Instruct the students to write, review, or revise in pairs, small groups, or as a whole group. Do this often. Lead students through a part of the process. Give them short tasks. Tell them what to look for, consider, circle, add, or revise. Your students will become accomplished at the process, and then they'll be able to do it alone.

9 **Ask good questions.** Consistently ask students questions that inspire and require critical thinking about writing (their own and others'). This will help them improve their skills in all stages of the writing process. Along the way, you'll demonstrate to students how to question and what types of questions to ask themselves when writing.

Ask such questions as:
- *What is the author's main point? What details in the text support that idea?*
- *What did the writer do well? How can you tell? What grabbed you?*
- *What is unique about the way the writer uses language?*
- *What did the writer do to ensure that the message got across?*
- *What line will you probably remember (or would you like to hear again)? Why?*
- *What is the writer's attitude about the subject? How can you tell?*
- *What parts of the text convinced you the most of the author's viewpoint?*
- *How did the writer use figurative language (or any other device) to accomplish the purpose?*
- *What kinds of sentences does the writer use? What effect does that have?*
- *Which phrases "paint" a picture for you? Precisely how does the writer accomplish this?*
- *What can you tell about the writer's personality? How can you tell this?*
- *What do you notice about the organization of the writing? How does it help get the point across?*
- *What was powerful (or ordinary) about the beginning? . . . the ending?*

10 **Teach mini-lessons on specific techniques.** Separate out individual skills and techniques to plan specific instruction on such topics as:

- creating fantastic beginnings
- crafting satisfying, creative endings
- improving beginnings, details, or conclusions
- writing clear theses
- writing details to support main ideas
- replacing ordinary words with more interesting ones
- identifying elements of voice in different passages
- putting your own voice into the writing
- "showing" rather than "telling" the reader
- adding specific literary devices to a passage
- eliminating unnecessary words, phrases, ideas
- rearranging ideas for clearer meaning
- varying form and content to fit different purposes
- experimenting with different structural approaches
- changing repetitive or boring sentence beginnings
- experimenting with sentence rhythm
- expanding an idea with better evidence
- adding figurative language
- adding anecdotes
- adding dialogue
- active verbs
- better transitions
- great topic sentences
- specific genres and modes
- specific stages of the writing process
- specific literary elements
- specific writing devices
- sensible sequence and organization
- strong titles, captions, headlines
- varied kinds of sentences or varied sentence lengths and structures
- capitalization and punctuation
- grammar and usage
- paragraphing

Revision Checklist

Focus on a few items to revise at a time. Don't try to revise all of the suggestions below at the same time or in a single piece of writing.

_____ Add or substitute words that are fresher, richer, more original, more energizing, more active, more fitting to the context, or more convincing.

_____ Eliminate repetitive or unnecessary words or ideas.

_____ Remove excess adjectives and adverbs.

_____ Add words or phrases that create a certain mood.

_____ Rearrange words within a sentence for meaning.

_____ Rearrange words or sentences for smoother flow.

_____ Expand sentences to include more detail.

_____ Include details and examples that are relevant and rich.

_____ Add details that "show" instead of "tell" the reader.

_____ Rearrange sentences for clarity, a different meaning, or better sequence.

_____ Rearrange sentences for more interesting sound or rhythm.

_____ Rework organization to clarify the meaning.

_____ Vary sentence structure, length, and rhythm.

_____ Break up excessively long sentences.

_____ Replace weak titles with strong, "catchy" titles.

_____ Replace ordinary beginnings with smashing beginnings.

_____ Make endings more memorable.

_____ Strengthen and vary transitions; make sure they are smooth.

_____ Rework to strengthen voice (*i.e., liveliness, originality, personality, conviction, author involvement, authenticity, good communication with audience*).

_____ Include literary techniques (*e.g., understatement, exaggeration,* or *foreshadowing*).

_____ Add figurative language.

_____ Clarify or expand main ideas.

_____ Add dialogue where it would be effective.

_____ Add or sharpen details to support main ideas or claims more powerfully.

_____ Examine for correct conventions (*spelling, punctuation, capitalization, paragraphing, grammar, usage*).

From Start to Finish

Follow the 10 steps to complete the writing process.

Name _____ Date _____

Topic or idea _____

Step 1 **Romancing:** This writing was inspired by:

Step 2 **Collecting:** Words, phrases, thoughts, facts, questions, or observations on the topic:

Step 3 **Organizing:** I've made a web for organizing the writing. The main ideas:

I have sufficient details to support each main idea.   *Yes   No*

Step 4 **Drafting:** I've written my rough draft. The strongest part:

Step 5 **Reviewing (by myself):** Two things I learned from my review:

Step 6 **Sharing for Response:** Two things I learned from others who reviewed my work:

Step 7 **Sharing for Response:** Two improvements I made:

Step 8 **Checking Conventions:** I've inspected the draft for spelling, grammar, mechanical, and structural errors. One error I corrected is:

Step 9 **Polishing:** I am satisfied with my polished draft.   *Yes   No*

Step 10 **Presenting:** I plan to share or show off my polished writing in this way:

Argumentative Writing

Argumentation is the art of using words (perhaps supplemented by other forms of communication) to convince an audience of a viewpoint or idea. It is the process of stating a clear position and supporting it with well-reasoned, strong evidence.

Argumentation is a central component of Common Core State Standards and other college- and career-ready state standards. Students need to hone the skills of argumentation and use them to investigate a claim or position, find credible evidence that supports it or refutes it, reach reasoned conclusions, and present a clear argument. The ability to argue well is essential for all content areas.

Why teach the argumentation process?

- Argumentation hones critical thinking skills that serve students well in all subject areas.

- Through the argumentation process, students practice forming, defending, and adjusting their own judgments and opinions.

- The dialogue and give-and-take involved in argumentation, particularly debate, give students a wonderful chance to clarify their own thinking and test their reasons against the claims and reasoning of others.

- Students are bombarded by all kinds of messages from a myriad of sources (in print, online, from media presentations, in social settings and communication) in this complex world. Argumentation skills are defensive tools to help them guard against fallacies or manipulation and find the truth.

With the technology now available to students, there are countless places and reasons to craft and present effective arguments. Stretch beyond the ordinary uses of argumentation (formal debates and written arguments) by using different types of technological devices and programs to gather ideas about positions to argue and details to support a position. Give students ample opportunities to present and respond to arguments in global-sharing settings, multimedia presentations, social media communications, and dozens of other settings made possible by technology. (See pages 8 through 11 for technology-connection ideas for language arts learning.)

Get Prepared to Argue

Choose your topic. Then follow this plan.

1 Prepare your introduction.

- Warm up the audience with a *hook*—something to immediately catch their attention, such as a quote, a shocking fact, a visual or spoken anecdote, a startling statistic, or anything else that grabs their interest.

- State your **CLAIM**. State or write in a single sentence, clearly and convincingly, your one major idea.

Types of claims:

> **Factual Claims** draw conclusions about relationships or conditions.
> *Example: Climate change has been accelerating more rapidly in the past ten years than at any other time in history.*
>
> **Value Claims** judge the merit of a process, practice, idea, or object based on specific criteria that the author or speaker suggests. They usually offer a positive or negative view of the topic.
> *Example: The Internet is a dangerous tool for teenagers.*
>
> **Policy Claims** call for change in behavior or policy or make a point that a particular action is needed.
> *Example: Schools need dress codes.*

- Include a narration—a summary of background information and definitions that readers or listeners need to know to set the issue in context.

By the end of the introduction, your audience should be captivated, know the claim, and have a sense of what is at stake with this issue.

2 Prepare the confirmation of your claim.

- Logically lay out the evidence that supports the claim. Use reasoning that links the evidence to the claim. Prepare well-informed and believable arguments.

- Take each point in the argument and support it with facts, examples, and testimony.

- Use strong, credible evidence from reliable sources. Without strong and trustworthy evidence, your argument becomes an opinion piece.

- Set up a chain of reasoning to build, build, build your argument. Each part of this section should add strength to your argument. Move from statements the audience will likely accept (evidence) to the proposition that is disputable or controversial (your claim).

3 Prepare to handle opposing viewpoints.

- Let the audience know any opposing viewpoints you accept (concede).

- Anticipate any objections to your viewpoint (opposing claims or alternative claims). Summarize them briefly. State them clearly and fairly.

- Then, show how opposing viewpoints are wrong or how the reasoning is flawed. Refute them, point by point, with strong evidence. Use the "Yes, but . . . " phrase. Taking each point, one at a time, concede the viewpoint (that's the "yes" part) and refute the point (that's the "but" part).

- Show how your argument goes farther, applies to a larger number, or is better.

4 Wrap it up with a good summation (conclusion).

- Restate your argument in a fresh way (not an exact restatement of your claim).

- Remind your audience of the importance of the issue.

- Reinforce the reasons your claim is the right viewpoint or best solution.

- This is your last chance. Make your argument absolutely convincing! Leave listeners, viewers, or readers with something they will remember.

A Few Hot Topics to Argue (for either side of a claim)

- Middle and high school students should be allowed to use cell phones at school.
- The Internet is harmful for children and young adolescents to use.
- Virtual reality should not be used for entertainment.
- Celebrities make poor role models.
- It is never good to keep secrets.
- Any student who cheats should be expelled from school.
- Students should be invited to all parent-teacher conferences.
- Use of social media sites is detrimental to developing real relationships.
- Every country has the right to develop nuclear power.
- Technology has negative influences on society.
- It is necessary to sacrifice some civil liberties for the promise of security.
- Dress codes violate the rights of students.

Build an Argument

Topic and source _____

Audience _____

Appeals I will use (logos, pathos, ethos):

Introduction
Hook:

Claim:

Confirmation

Evidence	Reasoned Connections
•	•
•	•
•	•
•	•

Handling Opposing Viewpoints

Viewpoint	Objection or Refutation

Summation
Ideas:

Memorable last sentence:

Name _____ Date_____

Student Scoring Guide for Writing

	5	3	1
Ideas	• Clear, extraordinary ideas, focused on the main point • Several specific, interesting details that support the key idea • Clear evidence of purpose and audience • Writing "shows" (rather than "tells")	• Ideas and main points are mostly clear and focused • Some general or ordinary details to support main point • Mostly clear purpose and audience • Attempt to "show" ideas	• Unclear ideas; ordinary content • Few or no supporting details • Unclear purpose and/or audience • Little "showing" of main points
Organization	• Powerful and satisfying beginning and ending • Sensible sequence; clear direction • Structure that helps to make the meaning clear • Smooth transitions	• Clear (though somewhat ordinary) beginning and ending • Clear, sensible sequence • Predictable story or idea path • Workable transitions	• Unclear beginning and/or ending • Confusing sequence • Awkward story path • Main point hard to find • Missing or clumsy transitions
Words	• A variety of precise, fresh, interesting words • Sensory appeal; active verbs • No overused words; careful and minimal use of adjectives and adverbs	• Mostly effective, accurate word use • Some sensory appeal; some active verbs • Some ordinary or overused words or misuse of jargon	• Limited, ordinary, vague, or inaccurate vocabulary • Writing does not paint a picture or appeal to senses • Few active verbs used
Sentences	• Sentences flow smoothly with interesting rhythm • Varied sentence types, lengths, and structures	• Mostly smooth sentences with interesting sounds • Some variety in sentence types, lengths, and structures	• Poor sentence flow • Little variety in sentence types, lengths, and structures
Voice	• Writer's self shows • Evidence of passion and flair • Directness, honesty	• Writer's self shows • Evidence of honesty and feeling • Some stiffness or insincerity	• Shows little or no sense of who the writer is • Little or no feeling or energy
Conventions	• Correct conventions • Correct grammar and language usage	• Few errors in conventions or grammar and language usage • Minor errors that do not affect the meaning	• Many errors in conventions or grammar and language usage • Errors that interfere with communication of the message

Chapter 5

Spark Writing, Speaking, and Discussion with Prompts

Practical Tips and Prompts for Many Tasks

by Peri Sandifer

Using Prompts

This chapter includes over 100 timely and thought-provoking prompts. Use them to:
- wake up the most lackadaisical student
- practice and develop writing, speaking, and organizational skills
- inspire students to think, analyze, and synthesize information
- give students practice in supporting claims and positions with relevant evidence
- assess student understanding

Each prompt requires students to analyze what is being asked or proposed and to respond in a thorough, organized manner in written or oral form. These prompts will spur your students' thinking and pursuit of evidence. Use them for discussions, debates, individual speeches, essay writing, audio presentations, visual presentations, or oral performances in any content area.

When using prompts, think beyond the traditional written essay, speech, or discussion by using available technology to gather information, plan, organize, and construct a presentation or discussion. Offer a selection of digital tools and programs, and encourage students to find innovative ways to create, share, reflect upon, and respond to their work. (See pages 8 through 11 for technology-connection ideas.)

Use prompts in any content area. For example:

In science — Begin a discussion of scientific advancements with a prompt:
> *Science is revolutionary! How do scientific advancements change society for better or for worse? Use specific examples to explain your position.*

In social studies — Use a prompt to introduce one aspect of government and to connect the lesson to students' lives:
> *During election campaigns, candidates often use such tactics as "mudslinging" or "spinning" to make their opponents look bad. If you were to run for mayor against a friend or close acquaintance and you knew your opponent's darkest secret, would you use the knowledge against him or her? Explain your answer.*

Follow That Prompt!

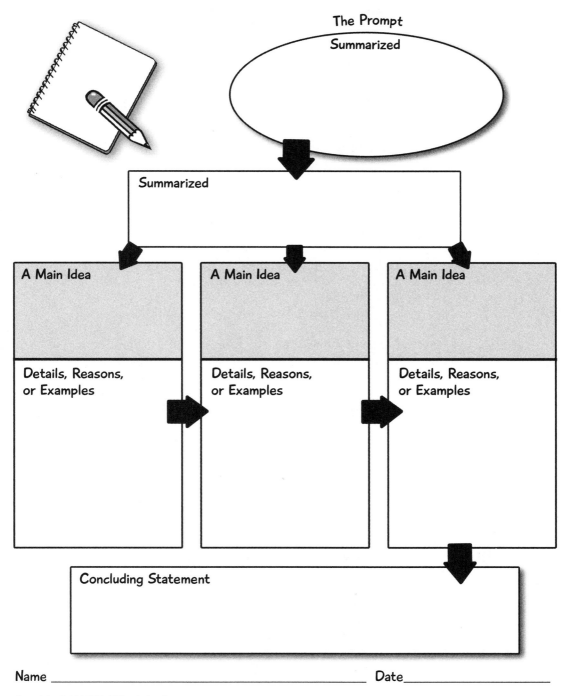

The Prompt
Summarized

Summarized

A Main Idea

Details, Reasons, or Examples

A Main Idea

Details, Reasons, or Examples

A Main Idea

Details, Reasons, or Examples

Concluding Statement

Name _____ Date_____

Inspire Creative Thinking

Cultivate your students' creative thinking skills by using these prompts for practice in expository, narrative, argumentative, or descriptive writing; speaking; discussions; or multimedia presentations.

1 You doze for a moment during your English teacher's introduction to a Shakespeare play. You look up and discover that the teacher is dressed as a king and is speaking with a British accent. Alas! You begin to realize that you are within the setting of the Shakespeare play, and you are one of the characters. Describe your character and the role you take in creating the story line (even if it is different from what Shakespeare wrote).

2 Choose any two superheroes. Imagine that their powers are combined into one mega superhero. Gather with at least two classmates who have envisioned their own mega superheroes. In your group, discuss what might occur when each new superhero tries to rescue someone or intervene in a dangerous or disastrous situation. Prepare a group speech or dramatization of your ideas.

3 You made this wish on a shooting star: "I wish that I would automatically know everything being taught this week in my science class and that I would not have to study." Your wish came true! How does this change your school experience?

4 Choose an interesting word. Write a speech, story, poem, advice column, article, or description that includes that word. But wait! Your task is to minimize the importance of the word! As you write the piece, purposely hide the word in your text. Your readers will have the task of identifying the original word that inspired the piece. You want their detecting task to be difficult!

5 You are headed to school, but as you turn into the well-worn parking lot, you notice that there are no cars. When you try to enter the building, you find it locked. A sign says the school has moved, but does not tell where. Describe your efforts to locate the school.

6 You are settled in for the evening, picking up a book to help you nod off to sleep. To your amazement, you gradually suspect that one of the main characters in the book is you! What explicit or implicit characteristics lead you to believe that the main character is you?

7 Overnight, 100 pizzas baked for a charity pizza-eating contest were stolen! The police are searching to find the thief. Your footprints and jacket have been discovered at the scene of the crime. You claim you didn't do it. Give your alibi and an explanation as to why your footprints and jacket were found at the scene.

8 Design or create a new technological device and a marketing pitch to sell it. Give the pitch to a small or large group (or record and post it online)!

9 This morning, you awoke to find that you no longer have feet! Flippers are now in place at the ends of your legs. How does this change your daily activities?

10 It is the year 2050. What technological advancements have occurred since 2015? (Name two.) How have they changed life for people?

11 A famous literary character from a well-known novel has appeared to you and asked you to help change the novel's storyline. How will you change it? How will this affect the outcome of the story?

12 It seems to be an ordinary day. You are sitting in class and the teacher speaks; however, you hear nothing but gibberish. You can't understand your teacher or your classmates. How does this affect you and your activities? What do you do to understand the material taught that day?

13 Create a radically different menu for the school cafeteria. What is the reaction of the other students to your menu?

14 You have a dream of a new invention that will reshape society. What is the invention? In what ways will it positively change society?

15 You are asked to speak at a national conference for teen leadership. What will be the topic of your speech? Why did you choose this topic?

16 You have the opportunity to "rewrite" history. What part would you want to rewrite?

17 You no longer read books in school. Everything is recorded or sent by text message to your cell phone. Will this help or hurt your education? Explain your answer.

18 You are in a "race against time." How will you beat time?

19 You have awakened to discover that the color blue no longer exists. How does this change life as you know it?

20 You have won two tickets to a movie premier. You and a friend pick up the tickets and walk through the door to the theater. When you enter, you notice that you are the only ones there. What do you discover about the mysterious theater?

Practice Analyzing and Synthesizing

Use these prompts to help your students practice gathering and organizing material in preparation for speeches, discussions, written essays, debates, or other presentations. Have the students make outlines that show their main ideas and details that reinforce each idea.

1 Many celebrities find it impossible to live a private life. Should they have the right to a private life? Give two examples from headlines today to support your answer.

2 Due to national security issues, more security measures have been taken in many countries. Do you believe the measures that are in place now offer security? Use statistics to support your answers.

3 Many people believe that advertising companies focus on younger children more than they should. Do you find this to be accurate? Support your answers with examples of advertisements you have viewed, heard, or read.

4 Some people believe violent video games lead players to commit acts of violence. Do you believe this is true? Support your belief by citing published research.

5 The First Amendment of the United States Constitution states the following: "Congress shall make no law respecting an establishment of religion, or prohibiting the free exercise thereof; or abridging the freedom of speech, or of the press; or the right of the people peaceably to assemble, and to petition the government for a redress of grievances." Do you believe that this amendment is respected today? Defend, challenge, or qualify your answer with examples from the news, magazines, or newspapers.

6 Albert Einstein once stated, "Imagination is more important than knowledge." Do you believe this to be true? Use examples from current events to defend or challenge your belief.

7 Some people believe that teens are overinvolved in school activities due to pressure from parents and from themselves. Do you believe this to be so? Defend your belief.

8 Some people say that higher education is not necessary for a successful life. Give specific examples to defend or challenge this belief.

9 Many people believe that technology makes day-to-day tasks easier to perform. Do you believe this to be so? Defend your belief.

10 Millions of people rely on technology every day. However, others believe that society depends too much on technology. Defend or challenge this view.

11 Social media networks, such as Facebook™ and Twitter®, are widely used by many teens and pre-teens. But, adults have many safety concerns about the use of such sites by young people. Give examples of some safety concerns and give responses or solutions to the concerns.

12 Today's teens have access to smartphones, laptop computers, tablets, and many other electronic gadgets. While all these gadgets are fun, are they hurting teens? Give examples in which you defend or challenge the belief that gadgets are hurting teens.

13 Cloning, stem cell research, and DNA testing represent major scientific advancements. Many believe such scientific progress will be used to harm rather than help society. Give specific evidence to challenge or defend this belief related to one of the three topics identified above.

14 Identify at least one of the moral codes recognized by your society. Give examples in which you have seen this moral code applied, and then defend or challenge the code.

15 Prejudices exist in society. Give an example of a prejudice you have witnessed in your society. What solutions can you give to this prejudice?

16 In the United States court system, a person is innocent until proven guilty. Do you believe this ideal exists? Defend or challenge this claim.

17 Many students are focused on receiving a specific letter grade in each class and pressure themselves to achieve a certain grade. What are some causes of this situation? Give some solutions that could help lessen the focus on letter grades.

18 Some teens choose or need to work in addition to attending school. List the pros and cons of working while in school. Give and support your opinion about teens going to school and working.

19 Music permeates the lives of many teens and preteens in today's society. However, some people believe that lyrics to many songs might encourage listeners to act or think in a destructive manner. Think of songs that fit or defy this belief. Using specific examples, defend or challenge the idea that music can help lead young people down a destructive path.

20 Peer pressure is a common problem for young people. Give examples of instances in which you may have faced peer pressure, and offer solutions to the problem of dealing with the pressure young people face.

Craft a Strong Argument

Use these prompts to help students with argumentative writing or speaking, for debate preparation, or for any other presentation whose purpose is to convince an audience of a viewpoint. Instruct students to defend their positions with reliable and verifiable examples and evidence.

1 Obesity is a leading cause of preventable death in the United States. Who should be held responsible for the deaths—the individuals who are obese or those advertising and selling fattening foods?

2 Many people believe that boys and girls are stereotyped. For instance, people might reference the stereotype that boys are better at math than girls. Do you believe that statements like this one affect the performance of boys or girls in school?

3 If a teenager drops out of high school, should his or her driver's license be revoked by the state?

4 When celebrities get in trouble, should they receive a punishment that is harsher or more lenient than that given to regular citizens? In explaining your answer, cite at least two cases to support your position.

5 If someone breaks the law for the betterment of society, should he or she face punishment?

6 Some parents believe that movies with characters who smoke cigarettes should be rated "R." Do you agree?

7 Do extracurricular activities in school overpower or boost students' studies?

8 Many states have enacted a curfew for minors. Do you believe this helps keep kids safe?

9 In many cities and states, a person who talks on a cell phone while driving can be given a ticket. Do you agree with these laws?

10 Do universities put too much emphasis on standardized test scores as a measure of admitting an applicant as a student?

11 Do you believe written tests measure one's knowledge and abilities?

12 Should advertisers have the right to market products that are known to be harmful to consumers?

13 A wife asks her husband of 50 years to end her life because she is in the final stages of terminal cancer and has no hope for an improved quality of life. The husband responds out of his immense love for her and acts upon her wishes. But he is later sentenced to prison. Do you think he should be?

14 If the courts release a criminal and the criminal commits another crime, who should be held responsible—the individuals who released him or the criminal?

15 Should schools implement random drug testing on their students? Defend your position with examples from current events.

16 Should the length of time students attend high school be shortened to two years?

17 Does the news media focus too much on negative world events? How does this outlook affect society?

18 Do you believe limits should be placed on what is published on the Internet? If so, what should be the limits? If not, give specific examples and explain why not.

19 Einstein said, "Only a life lived for others is worth living." Do you agree with this statement?

20 Many people believe private citizens should not be allowed to own firearms. Do you agree or disagree?

21 Should all states outlaw the use of cell phones by persons who are driving?

22 Homework policies raise controversy in many schools. Should homework be banned for any grade levels?

23 Should Washington D.C. become a state?

20 Many school districts are banning soda machines from their schools. Should this ban extend to all schools?

Make and Support a Decision

Use these prompts to help students prepare for a discussion and to perform reflective journaling, speech preparation, essay writing, or any other presentation whose purpose involves making or explaining a decision. Instruct students to support their decisions with reliable examples or evidence.

1   Do all people in your society have freedom of speech?

2   Are there times that you are not respected because of your age?

3   In some countries, not all people have a right to an education. If that were the case for you, how would not attending school affect your life?

4   What law is not currently in place that you would like to see passed by the government?

5   Many people like to play jokes on others. When has a joke gone too far?

6   What is worse: drinking alcohol or using drugs?

7   Is there a better solution to a world controversy than war?

8   Does a person's name affect his or her employability?

9   Who should set the guidelines for how people should look or act?

10   Are ratings for movies still appropriate?

11   How many drinking and driving offenses should a person be allowed before he or she is sent to jail?

12   Obesity is a problem in our society. What are some ways that the government can help control this health problem?

13   Are the penalties for teenagers who smoke or drink severe enough to sway them from engaging in these behaviors?

14   What do you think could be a leading cause for teenagers dropping out of high school?

15   Many people give presents for such different reasons as holidays and birthdays. What if you were to give presents that the recipient couldn't touch, such as happiness or love? What and to whom would you give these abstract presents?

16   How does money change and influence the world?

17   If government did not exist, how would the world be different?

18   If you could relive one day in your life, what day would you relive? Why?

19   Many people believe that you can learn from your mistakes. From which mistakes have you learned? How did you learn from them?

20 A picture is worth a thousand words. Think of a picture you have taken or remember seeing. How is it "worth a thousand words"?

21 Many people believe that knowledge is power. How can knowledge be used in a positive or negative way to show its power?

22 If you had the ability and means to accomplish one great task, what would you do?

23 Is it better to be a leader or a follower? Why?

24 Are you a *spontaneous* person or a *predictable* person?

25 You overhear a friend planning to do or tell something that will harm another friend's reputation. Will you tell the other friend?

26 Would you take an offer of one million dollars if it meant losing your relationship with your best friend?

27 If you witnessed a crime (such as an assault or robbery) and you realized you knew the perpetrator, would you reveal that person's name to the police?

28 If a scientific advancement allowed you the opportunity to be smarter or taller, would you try the process—even if it posed some health risks?

29 If your town has a law that prohibited texting, would you comply with the law?

30 A man jumped onto the subway tracks to save a stranger who had fallen onto the tracks while experiencing a seizure. The rescuer held the stranger tight as the train went over them. His actions saved the stranger's life. Would you be willing to risk your life for a stranger's life?

31 You see a student being bullied. This student is not someone you know; however, you realize that what is being said and done is wrong. Are you willing to take a risk and try to stop the bullying?

32 Your best friend has asked you to help her cheat on a test, because if she doesn't pass this test, then she will fail the class. Will you help your friend cheat?

33 You know a friend has an eating disorder. You confront your friend with the evidence, and he asks you not to tell, promising he will do better with his eating habits. Will you keep his secret or tell someone?

34 A new student has arrived in class and some kids are beginning to make fun of him or her. Will you join in or befriend the new student?

35 You have witnessed your best friend stealing money from your mother's purse. Will you tell your mother, confront your friend, or let the act go?

Chapter 6

Sharpen Speaking and Listening Skills

Practical Tips to Help Teachers Nurture Effective Speakers and Active Listeners

by Marjorie Frank

Teaching for Effective Speaking and Listening

Speaking is the art of expressing and exchanging ideas with other persons in public or private. Oral communication goes far beyond the words that are spoken. It includes the ability to prepare, analyze, and deliver information, ideas, opinions, and other messages through verbal, vocal, and visual interactions. It involves emotions, attitudes, and personal responses.

Listening is far more than just hearing (understanding enough of an auditory message to get a general idea of what is being said). Listening involves the skill of understanding the message clearly, analyzing, or evaluating it, and connecting it to other information and experiences.

Student Expectations

- to be able to gain, analyze, organize, and prepare information, ideas, opinions, and other messages from a variety of sources for individual speaking, conversation, or collaboration

- to deliver ideas and messages through vocal, verbal, and visual interactions with others in a way that can be understood by an audience

- to focus attention on a speaker and the speaker's message and listen without interrupting, maintaining appropriate attention span, verbal responses, and body language

- to actively listen—process information, form questions, see connections to other information, summarize, respond, and make reasoned judgments

- to evaluate a speaker's presentation—including his or her use of rhetoric, gestures, reasoning, point of view, and use of evidence

> **Think beyond the soapbox!**
> The technology available to today's students pushes the processes of speaking and listening to exciting new places. Be sure that your students have opportunities to speak, listen, and discuss in many different situations, including multimedia presentations, dramas, TV or radio shows, videos, podcasts, social media communications, and a host of interactive digital apps and programs. (See pages 8 through 11 for technology-connection ideas for language arts learning.)

Speaking Activities

Why? *to share, inform, summarize, wonder, question, persuade, teach, provoke thought, reflect, critique*

Where? *in the classroom, in the hall, outdoors, at school events, in podcasts or webcast*

To or with whom? *the class, a student partner, a small group, other classes, online audiences, or discussion groups*

When? *anytime . . . OFTEN*

What? *formal speeches or informal speeches, planned speeches or impromptu speeches, conversations or collaborations of many kinds and purposes, for example:*

- interpretative talk
- cause-and-effect talk
- comparison-contrast talk
- book or story talk
- information talk
- art or music talk
- argument
- personal experience
- personality profile

- concept explanation
- how-to talk
- series of questions
- short critique
- mini-teaching lesson
- reflection
- narration
- summary
- text-section review

- map talk
- response to presentation
- someone else's viewpoint
- show-and-talk demonstration
- planning session
- decision-making session
- presentation analysis
- opinion sharing
- evaluation of any presentation

Handling Speech Anxiety
- Understand that everyone gets nervous.
- Choose a topic that will captivate your audience.
- Research the topic well.
- Prepare the topic well.
- Use some visual aids with your speech.
- Practice the speech over and over.
- Before the speech, relax by taking deep breaths, listening to soothing music, or doing some mild exercise to release tension.

Good-Speaker Tips

A good speaker DOES . . .

- identify the audience and the purpose of the speech.
- consider his or her attitude about the topic.
- think about how body language will affect the message.
- consider questions or objections the listeners might have.
- understand each part of the speech:

    Introduction — Tell the audience what information you will be sharing with them.

    Body — Tell them the information.

    Conclusion — Tell them what information you just shared with them.

- choose a topic that interests her or him.
- know what he or she wants to say.
- understand and respect the audience.
- use humor where appropriate.
- understand and research the topic well.
- present adequate, reliable evidence to support a point of view or claim.
- plan each section of the speech well.
- consider how to use nonverbal communication to convey the message.
- practice the speech.
- show enthusiasm for the topic and presentation.

A good speaker DOES NOT . . .

- choose a topic that will be of little interest to the audience.
- choose a topic that is inappropriate for the audience or the occasion.
- give a disorganized speech.
- use overly complex vocabulary or long, involved sentences.
- include jargon, slang, or offensive jokes.
- mumble or speak too quietly or loudly.
- fidget, wiggle, pace, or stand stiff like a statue.
- ignore or insult the audience.
- focus on just one person in the audience.
- present in an overly casual or arrogant tone.
- apologize for any part of the speech or its presentation.

Preparing a Speech

1. Choose a topic.
Select a topic that is familiar, important, or interesting to you. Think about what matters to you and your audience.

2. Decide on your purpose.
Why are you giving the speech? What do you hope to accomplish?

3. Identify your audience.
Think about who is in the audience, what might be appropriate to their level of understanding and interests, and what they might already know about the topic.

4. Gather information.
Write down everything you know about the topic. If you need to know more, do some research and consult several sources, including people. Find strong, reliable evidence to support your ideas, point of view, or claims. Carefully take notes on key ideas, facts, and questions. Also, look for specific quotes or statistics you might want to include as support for your topic.

5. Organize your material.
Sort your notes into categories or subcategories. Place them in a sensible sequence.

6. Plan the timing.
Know how much time you have for the speech. Think about how much time you will use to deliver the introduction, the body, and the conclusion of the speech.

7. Write the body of the speech.
Describe each key idea clearly. Give relevant, creative, and interesting examples to support each idea.

Don't overwhelm the audience with too many statistics or facts. Use concrete details that paint a picture for the listeners.

Write with language that is creative but not difficult.

Choose language that reflects your own voice and passion for the topic.

Write smooth transitions between ideas.

8. Write a strong introduction.
Start with a sentence that grabs the audience's attention! Use a startling fact, a funny anecdote, a great quote, an interesting question, or a strong statement designed to arouse the audience's curiosity or emotions. Somewhere in your introduction, clearly state the purpose and main point of your speech in terms the audience can understand.

9. Write a memorable conclusion.

Finish with a bang! End your speech by making sure your audience understands the main message. Make your final statements energetic! Leave the listeners satisfied, inspired, and ready to act.

10. Prepare your note cards.

Write enough notes on your cards so that they will be helpful. Do not try to write your entire speech word-for-word on the cards. You may choose to only write the main points and one or two key words for each supporting point. Place the cards in proper sequence and number them to avoid confusion if they should get out of order.

11. Prepare your visual aids.

Create visual aids that will complement your presentation, such as charts, posters, objects, electronic presentation slides, music, photographs, etc. Carefully think about how and when you will use each aid. You want them to add to your speech, not distract from it or overshadow it.

12. Memorize your introduction and conclusion.

As a strategy to reduce speech anxiety, many presenters memorize both the introduction and conclusion word-for-word. Having these parts memorized helps you to create interest in your opening and present a memorable ending for your audience.

13. Practice. Practice. Practice.

Rehearse your speech in front of a mirror, a friend, a video camera, or an audio recorder. Before the final speech, watch and listen to the recorded speech to see what you could improve.

14. Present with confidence!

When it's time to present, remember to maintain confidence in your practiced skills and deep knowledge of the topic!

Giving an Effective Speech

Preparing a great speech is just the beginning. The rest of the task is polishing your delivery skills. Check this list, again and again, before you give your speech. These practices should come to be a natural part of your delivery.

✓ **Confidence** – You've planned and practiced your speech. You are ready. Believe that you know your topic well. Also believe that the audience wants to hear your ideas and is wishing you well as you present them.

✓ **Posture** – Stand up straight, but not stiff. Don't slouch, pace, or sway back and forth from foot to foot. Move a bit. This will keep you relaxed and stave off the jitters.

✓ **Language** – Talk as if you are having a conversation with a friend. Speak in language you are comfortable with. Use short, active sentences, but don't let the delivery become choppy. Speak clearly. Make smooth transitions from one idea to the next.

✓ **Volume** – Speak up. Don't whisper, don't shout, but speak loudly enough so that everyone can hear. Project your voice to the back of the room.

✓ **Speed** – Slow down. The most common speaking problem is talking too fast. Pay attention to your speed as the speech goes along. Many speakers have a tendency to speed up as they talk and start racing toward the end. Don't rush—at any point.

✓ **Pauses** – Pause now and then, particularly after making an important point. Pause a bit after your introduction and before your conclusion. If there is laughter or an interruption, pause until things quiet down. Then, begin where you left off.

✓ **Tone** – Use a natural, friendly tone. Avoid sounding timid or hesitant. Avoid being too casual and chatty. Avoid sounding impersonal. Avoid a monotone sound.

✓ **Language** – Use facial expressions and gestures carefully and naturally to emphasize important points. Don't overdo it.

✓ **Hands** – Make a plan for your hands. Don't let them dangle awkwardly by your sides, or use them to scratch your head, pull on your hair, or drum on the desk. Try not to talk with your hands too much. Try to relax them and use them naturally.

✓ **Enthusiasm** – Speak with enthusiasm for your topic and conviction about your ideas.

✓ **Rapport** – Speak directly to your audience. Maintain eye contact with them at all times. Scan the room, allowing your gaze to linger for a few seconds on various individuals. If someone is distracting to you or makes you laugh, avoid looking at that person.

✓ **Completion** – Leave the audience with a positive impression. Use a strong voice to end your speech. Finish what you have to say, and then sit down. Don't linger at the front of the room. Make sure the audience knows that you are finished.

Speech Response: Peer Feedback

Speaker _____ Topic _____

Responder _____ Date _____

Overall Impression: _____

_____

What I noticed about the beginning and/or conclusion of your speech: _____

_____

What I learned from your speech: _____

_____

A comment about **what** you said (*how it grabbed my interest, developed a main point, supported the ideas, appealed to the audience; how easy it was to follow*):

A comment about **how** you said it (*language usage, speed, energy, clarity, body language, rapport with the audience, comfort and naturalness of the delivery*):

A compliment _____

_____

A suggestion: _____

_____

Student Scoring Guide for Speaking

Use this guide for self-scoring or peer scoring a speech.

Content	Score 5	Score 3	Score 1
• The speech showed that the speaker was familiar and comfortable with the topic. • The purpose and main ideas were clear and focused. • The purpose and main ideas were appropriate for the audience. • The main idea was strongly supported with clear, interesting, and relevant evidence and details. • The ideas were creative, fresh, and interesting.	*Highly successful: criteria reached consistently, strongly, effectively, and convincingly*	*Mostly successful, but included some generalities with moderate support*	*Minimally successful or lacking entirely*

Organization	Score 5	Score 3	Score 1
• The presentation was easy to follow. • The organization and sequence made sense. • The speech included a clear beginning, middle, and end. • The speech had a catchy introduction and a memorable conclusion that creatively summed up the message. • The speech had smooth transitions between ideas.	*Highly successful: criteria reached consistently, and effectively*	*Mostly successful*	*Hard to follow, minimally successful, or lacking entirely*

Language	Score 5	Score 3	Score 1
• The words chosen were interesting and expressive. • The words painted a picture for the audience. • Grammar was correctly used. • The speaker used the appropriate level of seriousness or humor for the topic.	*Highly successful: criteria reached consistently and effectively*	*Mostly successful*	*Minimally successful with several errors*

Delivery	Score 5	Score 3	Score 1
• The speaker kept eye contact with the audience. • The speed and volume of the delivery was appropriate. • The speaker spoke with energy and enthusiasm. • The speaking flowed along smoothly. • The speaker's body language helped get the message across and was not distracting. • The speaker seemed well prepared for the speech.	*Highly successful: criteria reached consistently and effectively*	*Mostly successful*	*Minimally successful or lacking entirely*

Listening Activities

Why? *to hear and understand a message*

Where? *in the classroom, at home, and everywhere you go*

When? *anytime, all the time*

To Whom? *each other, the teacher, media sources, various people or sources outside of school*

How? *actively and critically. Engage students in casual or formal activities during and after listening. Tell them what to listen for. Share criteria for good listening. Provide a way for some feedback: summarize, respond, or evaluate in small groups or pairs, using a checklist. Respond orally or in writing.*

What? *formal and informal presentations or assignments of many kinds, for example:*

- news reports
- video clips
- short speeches
- conversations
- jokes, puns, riddles
- short paragraphs
- mini-lectures or lessons
- dramas
- opinions

- arguments
- poetry
- demonstrations
- responses
- lyrics
- TV or movie clips
- stories
- multimedia presentations
- print and digital advertisements

- newspaper articles
- questions
- interviews
- summaries
- monologues
- explanations
- reviews

Good-Listener Tips

The purpose of listening is to learn something new, to analyze and examine it, to make sense of it, to connect it to your life and world, and to make use of it. Listening is a challenging mental task. Be ready to take on the challenge!

Before You Listen
- Learn something about the topic, if you can.
- INTEND to listen.
- Sit where you can see and hear.
- Sit away from distracting things or people.
- Stop talking.
- Be prepared to take notes, if needed.

As You Listen

- Look at the speaker to give your full attention. Focus on what is being said.
- Listen actively—with an open mind.
- Listen and watch for the main points, central themes, and deep meanings.
- Listen and watch for convincing, reliable evidence or details and examples to support the main points.
- Show respectful, appropriate responses.
- Watch for signals about what ideas are most important (e.g., the speaker's emphasis with the voice, repeated phrases, writing on the board or screen, handouts, visual aids, or the speaker's summary).
- Watch for such nonverbal cues as facial expressions and gestures that signal what ideas are important.
- Ask mental questions. *(What is the key message? What's the evidence? What should I remember? How does this fit with what I know or learned?)*
- Take detailed notes on key points.

After You Listen

- Ask questions to be sure you understood the main points.
- Give feedback to the speaker, if appropriate.
- Review. *(Ask yourself: So what? What difference does this make? What did I learn? What else would I like to know? How does this relate to other situations? How does this affect me?)*
- Write or record a summary of your understandings.

DON'T . . .

   . . . interrupt, make comments, or cause distractions.

   . . . talk, fidget, daydream, gaze around the room, or get distracted.

   . . . show impatience or disinterest with your body language.

   . . . tune out because the subject is not of high interest to you.

   . . . tune out if ideas get too difficult.

   . . . try to write down everything that's said.

   . . . focus on the speaker's delivery instead of the content.

   . . . judge the speaker's ideas too quickly and without thought.

   . . . judge the speaker's delivery unless you are asked to give feedback on it.

   . . . dismiss the speaker because you disagree with some ideas.

   . . . think so hard about what you are going to say or ask that you fail to hear what the speaker is saying.

   . . . give inappropriate responses, verbally or nonverbally.

Listener's Reflection

Use this form after you've listened to any presentation.

Speaker or Source _____ Topic _____

Listener _____ Date _____

What was the purpose of the presentation?

What did I hear? (Summarize the main points.)

What was most important?

What difference does this information make?

What affected the message (humor, body language, visuals, sound effects, etc.), and what was the impact?

Chapter 7

Log On and Inspire Savvy Internet Research and Evaluation

Practical Tips for Teaching Students to Find and Use Reliable Online Information

by Dr. Bill McBride

Find It! Evaluate It!

Finding, analyzing, evaluating, integrating, and applying information takes a set of skills critical to a student's academic success. In literally every subject area and learning venture, students will have opportunities (and requirements) to explore, investigate, locate, argue, write, debate, report, or design. They can't follow any of these pursuits without doing research, and today's students are unlikely to research a topic without visiting the Internet. Since they **will** and **should** do online research, they need to know how to do it properly. Rescue your students from the common three-step approach to Internet research: *Google it, cut it, paste it.* Make sure students are ready to do something other than copy and paste. Teach them how to use this amazing resource to find up-to-date, relevant information they can trust. Locating and evaluating websites and identifying reliable facts are **must-have** skills for this digital generation. Give students chances to practice these skills before they plunge into a research project.

Students use technology when they do Internet research. In the process of searching and examining sites, they'll undoubtedly have chances to use many other great tech processes as they research, collect, organize, and summarize information. Watch for opportunities for them to review video and audio clips, tap into blogs, seek and share information on a variety of sharing sites, send off tweets and texts, scan or create QR Codes, collaborate on research projects, publish their ideas and findings, and find real-world applications for their positions. (See pages 8 through 11 for technology-connection ideas for language arts learning.)

Steps for Internet Research

Step 1 Learn the language of Internet research.

These are some of the terms to know in order to understand and evaluate the information a researcher finds.

- **analyze** – examine all the parts of something
- **conclude** – come to broad understandings based on evidence gathered
- **counterevidence** – facts that support an opposite theory or position
- **data** – information that is collected
- **evaluate** – make judgments about the value or validity of something
- **evidence** – facts that support a theory or position
- **generalize** – make a guess about a broad concept based on limited information
- **mean** – the answer that results after adding all the numbers and dividing by the number of numbers
- **median** – number in the middle of a group of data
- **mode** – number that occurs the most often
- **percentage** – part or all of a group
- **population** – total number of people or items in a group
- **questionnaire** – a list of questions
- **range** – difference between the lowest and highest points in a group
- **sample** – a small part of a larger population
- **search engine** – a website that looks through millions of computer files for something
- **statistics** – facts in the form of numbers
- **survey** – to ask a group of people the same questions
- **URL (universal resource locator)** – a web address

Step 1 Practice

To practice use of research terms:

- Add them to the WORD WALL in your classroom. Discuss what you already know about the words or previous experiences you have had with the process or idea.
- Review definitions from different sources. Write a definition that is clear for YOU.
- Use the words repeatedly in many different ways over a period of several weeks.

Step 2 Use online reference sites and tools.

Now that you've chosen a topic, you (or you and a partner) will begin to do research to build an argument or take a position. You can find up-to-date information on the Internet. Here are some resources to investigate.

www.encyclopedia.com — Encyclopedia.com provides users with more than 57,000 frequently updated articles from *The Columbia Encyclopedia*. Each article is enhanced with links to newspaper and magazine articles, as well as pictures and maps.

www.infoplease.com/encyclopedia — This site also provides more than 57,000 frequently updated articles from *The Columbia Encyclopedia*, subdivided into the following categories: Earth and Environment; History; Literature and Arts; Medicine; People; Philosophy and Religion; Places; Plants and Animals; Science and Technology; Social Sciences and Law; and Sports and Everyday Life.

www.m-w.com — *The Merriam-Webster Dictionary* is online, and besides providing thousands of definitions, the site also has a Daily Crossword puzzle, a Daily Buzzword game, a Learner's Word of the Day, and for those learning English, a Daily Podcast.

www.bartleby.com — Bartleby is a publisher of literature and reference works. This all-inclusive site has *The Columbia Online Encyclopedia, The American Heritage Dictionary, Roget's II Thesaurus, Columbia Book of Quotations, Bartlett's Familiar Quotations, The Oxford Shakespeare, The King James Bible, Gray's Anatomy, The World Factbook,* and *Strunk's Elements of Style.*

www.factmonster.com — An excellent site for students aged six to fifteen, this site provides almanac and feature articles as well as encyclopedia and dictionary entries. The site also provides fun trivia and word games.

www.wikipedia.org — The good news about *Wikipedia* is that anyone can edit an article on this encyclopedia. Because things change so quickly in today's world, information can be constantly updated. Also, the articles are free content so that they may be reproduced freely without special permission. The bad news is that anyone can edit an article on this encyclopedia! So anyone can post incorrect information about a topic.

www.wolframalpha.com — This cool website is a computational knowledge engine that provides facts and data "across a range of topics, including science, nutrition, history, geography, engineering, mathematics." It is especially useful for math and science questions.

Other reference sites that require a subscription include: www.worldbookonline.com and www.britannica.com.

Step 2 Practice
To practice use of online resources:

- Look up your topic at *encyclopedia.com, Fact Monster™, Bartleby™,* and at least one other Internet site. If you can't find your topic on one site, then choose another site.

- Decide which of these sites seems to be the most valuable for finding the kind of information you need. Describe what you found that was helpful and explain why it was helpful.

- Ask your school librarian or a librarian at your public library for help if you can't find useful sources or have trouble using the sites you do find.

Step 3 Research with search engines.

Follow this advice to make the best use of the Internet for your research.

1. Choose key words about your subject. Ask yourself what the most important words related to your subject are and use these to begin your search. In the following examples, possible key words are printed in bold.

Action movies make greater profits than comedies.

Global warming can be solved with **alternative energy** sources.

Watch your punctuation. If you want to find EVERYTHING about **planets**, then type it in lower-case letters. In some search engines, if you type in **Planets**, you will get only responses with a capital letter.

2. Start your search engines. You have probably looked for things using Google™, Dogpile®, Ask Jeeves®, or DuckDuckGo®. These are search engines. Search engines are computer programs that look through thousands of electronic files to find the key words you have typed in. The problem with search engines is that they take you to ANY information related to your search. The site you choose may have accurate information, or it may contain incorrect information. For example, let's imagine that your topic is George W. Bush, the 43rd U.S. president. Below are two of the top websites that appear when you Google "George W. Bush." The first one is legitimate information about the former president, and the second site is a parody that includes spoof news, gossip, and false information.

http://www.whitehouse.gov/about/presidents/georgewbush
http://www.georgewbush.org

Use more than one search engine. While Google™, Yahoo®, or Dogpile® are good places to start, you will want to use other search engines to for serious research. Some good engines to try are https://duckduckgo.com, http://blekko.com, http://webcrawler.com, or http://excite.com.

Use quotation marks in your search. Type quotation marks around any phrases (more than one word). If you type in **Tim Howard**, you will get sites with either of the two words—not just those related to Tim Howard, the soccer goalie.

Type in **"Tim Howard"** to find only sites that have content about people named Tim Howard or "Tim Howard, goalie" to find things related to the USA soccer goalie Tim Howard.

3. **Narrow your search.** What if you are really interested in the White House during the War of 1812? Use a grouping search method called **Boolean searching.** Combine the two topics by typing "White House" and "War of 1812."

- To combine two or more topics, type: **"hamburgers" AND "hot dogs" AND "French fries."**
- To limit a topic, type: **"hamburgers" AND "hot dogs" AND NOT "French fries."**
- To widen a search, type: **"hamburgers" OR "hot dogs" AND "French fries."**

4. **Narrow your search some more.** Another way to limit your search is to use plus (+) and minus (–) signs. If there is a term in your search that you **must** have, then put a + sign directly in front of the term, without a space.

For example, type into the search box **"SF Giants" AND "Barry Bonds" +"70th home run"** to get sites about Barry hitting his 70th home run in one season. You can also stop connections a search engine might make. You may be researching Barry Bonds but are not interested in whether or not he took steroids to make him a better hitter. To limit your search, use a – sign.

For example, type into the search box **"SF Giants" AND "Barry Bonds" – "steroids"** to omit any articles that mention steroids.

5. **Set up an alert.** Some search engines allow you to set an **alert.** Google™, for instance, allows you to set a **Google Alert**™ for your subject. Each day you will receive a variety of current articles from many different sources and perspectives sent to your email account. You'll learn how to evaluate these different sources later in this chapter.

Step 3 Practice
To practice research with search engines:

- Do an Internet search that allows you to combine key words. This will limit search results to only those sources that contain both (or all of the key words).

- Ask your school librarian or a librarian at your public library for help if you can't find useful sources or have trouble using the sites you do find.

- Follow the instructions as you complete the following page: "Do a Boolean Search."

Reproduce this page at 120% for 8½ x 11 size.

DO A BOOLEAN SEARCH

1 Choose a subject.

Circle a category.

SPORTS   MOVIES   FASHION   MUSIC

2 Choose a specific topic.

Narrow the search to a specific topic within the category.

Examples:
Sports: soccer; LeBron James
Movies: animated movies; Jennifer Lawrence
Fashion: street fashion; Versace
Music: classical; Taylor Swift

My specific topic is:

3 Choose a search engine.

The search engine I chose is: _____

Specific topic I typed: _____

Number of responses: ____   URL of a favorite article: _____

Title of the favorite article: _____

4 Narrow your search.
Think of a second term and add it to your first topic with an "AND."
Example: LeBron James AND Miami

My topic:
  AND
Number of responses:

URL of a favorite article:

Title of favorite article:

5 Narrow your search more.
Think of a third term that will further narrow or eliminate some responses using a + (or a -) sign.
Example: LeBron James AND Miami + 2012

My topic:
  AND
Number of responses:

URL of a favorite article:

Title of favorite article:

Name _____   Date_____

Step 4 Evaluate websites before you use them.

Ask yourself these questions before you take information from a website to use as material for your project.

1. What kind of site is this?

Begin by looking at the ending, or domain, to the URL (the uniform record locator). Sites that end in **.edu** and **.gov** may be more trustworthy because they are created to share information. Sites ending in **.com** may be less accurate because they are created by companies who wish to sell things. The most common types of sites are:

.com a company trying to sell something

.edu a school, community college, college, or university

.gov a local, state, or national government institution

.info an organization that provides information

.mil a military organization

.net an Internet network source or provider

.org usually a type of not-for-profit organization

.biz usually a business

2. Who wrote this?

Find out who the author is. Reliable websites tell you who wrote the information. Be careful that you are not on a **personal page** website. Individuals who want to express their own views create personal pages. There are certain clues that you may be on a personal page. If you see a person's name in the URL, such as **bmcbride** or the words **people** or **users**, you are probably on a personal page. Also, if you see the tilde symbol (~) or the percent sign (%), you may be on a personal page.

Ask yourself the following questions to make sure the author is trustworthy:

- Are there signs that this is a personal page?

- What's the name of the author who wrote the information?

- Is there an email address, physical address, or phone number for the author?

- Is there a brief biography of the author, or are there any facts about the author's life that show why he or she is considered an expert?

- Is there information about whom the author works for?

3. Who published this?

Organizations or companies create most websites. Find out which organization created the website. Ask yourself these questions to evaluate the organization that created a website:

- *What is the URL domain (ending)?*
- *Does the site include the name of the sponsoring organization?*
- *What does the site's About Us statement or Home Page say about the organization's purpose?*
- *Why might this organization want to publish this information?*

4. When was this written?

In today's world, information changes constantly. The "age" of the information on a website is an important component in its validity. Check the history of a site by using www.archive.org. **If you use any information from a site, record the date you accessed it.** What you find today may not be true in a week or month. The reader needs to know when you found your information. Ask yourself these questions:

- *What date was the website created?*
- *When was the information posted?*
- *Has this information ever been updated?*
- *Do I believe that this information is still valid?*

5. What tone does the writer take?

By reading a small part of a website, you can tell a lot about its viewpoint. For example:

- If the text is funny, then the site is probably using humor to make fun of someone or something. Humorous sites are entertaining but may not present accurate information.

- If the tone is sarcastic or derisive, the purpose of the site may be to criticize viewpoints or discount opinions.

6. What sites are linked to this site?

You can check how correct or unbiased a site is by reviewing the sites to which it is linked. To do this, use the search engine www.dogpile.com. For example, to see what sites are linked to the International Reading Association at www.reading.org, go to a search engine and type **link:http://www.reading.org** into the search box. (To check the links to any site, type in **link:** before the URL with no spaces in the search box.) The first page listed will be the Home Page for the IRA. Below it will be listed all the sites that have linked themselves to the IRA.

Because reading is such a popular topic, you'll see that *Dogpile®* found about 31,000,000 links. **Remember to ask yourself the following questions when checking your site:**

- *What sites are linked to the site from which I'm getting my information?*
- *Does the linked site say something that no other site agrees with?*
- *Does the linked site reference other printed information, such as magazines, journal and newspaper articles, or books?*
- *Does the linked site take an extreme or radical view?*

7. Overall, how accurate or reliable is this source?

Use the questions on the following Website Evaluation Questionnaire to help evaluate the websites you visit when doing your research. At the end, review your answers to make a judgment about the trustworthiness of the site.

Step 4 Practice

To practice evaluating websites:

- Choose one or more websites that you think may provide information on your topic.
- Review the questions on pages 93, 94, and 95.
- For each website, complete the Website Evaluation Questionnaire on page 96.

Website Evaluation Questionnaire

Answer these questions for each website you consider. By the time you reach the final question, you should be able to make some judgment as to whether or not this is a site with information that is helpful and trustworthy to use as a part of the evidence you are building for your position.

What is the URL of the site?

What does the URL domain (ending) tell you about the site?

Is there any sign in the URL that this is a Personal Page?

Who is the author?

What is the author's organization or address?

For whom does the author work?

What organization sponsors the site?

Does the home page provide any biased or extreme information?

Why does this organization want to publish this information?

On what dates were the site and article created or updated?

Based on the article's date, do you think this information is still valid?

Is the tone of this site serious, funny, or satirical?

What source does the author give for the information?

Do any of the linked sites take a biased or extreme view?

Overall, do you feel you can trust the information on this site?

Name _____ Date_____

Step 5 Follow the Evidence!

Follow the Evidence!

Now that you have identified some trustworthy sites, you are ready to start the research to find evidence to support your opinion, position, or idea. It is important that you also pay attention to counterevidence, so that you are aware of the facts, opinions, and arguments against your position.

Use this form to take notes.
Use **ONE** sheet for **EACH** website from which you take information.

What opinion or position are you trying to support?

What is the URL address of this site?

What facts did you find at this source to *support* your idea?

What facts did you find at this source that *pose counterarguments* to your idea?

What scientific research, surveys, or quotes from experts did you find to *support* your idea?

What scientific research, surveys, or quotes from experts did you find to *counter* your idea?

What real-world examples did you find to *support* your idea?

What real-world examples did you find to *counter* your idea?

Name _____ Date_____

Chapter 8

Banish the Fear of Research Papers

*Practical Tips to Help Students Manage
Research Papers Successfully*

by Joy MacKenzie

To Write a Research Paper

Most students approach a research paper with fear and trembling. (This includes adult students!) No matter how clear the assignment or how exciting the topic, there is still a panic that sets in when it is time to begin. The most common response to this fear is procrastination. When the befuddled writer and researcher **does** get started, it is often with a vision of drudgery and a helter-skelter, dazed approach. As the wise and calm teacher, you can help students conquer the "Yikes! A research paper! Help!" panic by giving them tools that can make the process much easier to handle.

- Give the assignment well in advance of the due date.

- Set due dates for stages in the process, not just for the completed paper.

- Present the assignment **clearly** in writing and verbally.

- Help students choose appropriate, interesting topics (topics that actually can be done—not too narrow and not too broad).

- Make sure all students have access to the correct style guide required by your school. Familiarize students with the guide.

- Be particularly clear about the citation process expected.

- Give students a copy of the 10-step plan. Review all parts of it with them. Reinforce the importance of breaking the process into smaller chunks and of taking breaks.

- Review the helpful tips with students. (See pages 108-109 in this book.)

- Look for ways that students can use available technology (the Internet and more) to seek and share topic ideas, find and evaluate sources and information, receive feedback on their work, summarize or share the final paper, and comment on the work of classmates. (See pages 8 through 11 for technology-connection ideas for language arts learning.)

The 10-Step Plan

> Use this plan as a magic wand to shrink the assignment from MONSTROUS to MANAGEABLE.

Step 1: Understand the assignment—well!

- **Get the assignment in writing!** All students need to **see** a long, important assignment in writing—not just **hear** it.

- **Make notes and highlight or underline** as the teacher explains the assignment so that you understand all requirements fully. Note anything that puzzles you.

- **Reread the assignment TWICE**—out loud to yourself—to be sure you know what to do. Ask questions if you are confused. Ask them sooner rather than later.

- **Look again.** Use a set of colored pens or markers to highlight any other important information on the assignment page you will need to keep in mind. (For instance, notice such things as type style, font size, number of pages or words required, required style manual, requirements for headings, and kinds and number of sources required.)

- **Get a three-ring binder notebook** with pockets on the inside covers. Make a copy of your assignment. Punch holes in it and put it in the notebook to stay. Keep the other copy in a folder that you may carry easily to a library or elsewhere.

- **Create a calendar.** Make a calendar for the time-span between now and the final due date. Note all due dates that are part of the assignment. Check them twice! Add a paper copy to your notebook. Also, enter these dates on any digital calendars you use on your cell phone, tablet, or computer.

- **Next** (do this even if you think it sounds silly!), **count backwards on the calendar at least four or five days from each due date.** Using **bold, capital letters**, re-enter what is due in the "earlier" spaces. Erase the old "real" due dates. This protects you against unexpected deterrents to your work (such as sickness, sports playoff games, other papers or tests, a lost backpack, computer or printer emergencies, or dogs devouring your paper), so you can be sure to finish on time.

BRIGHT IDEA!

See if you can talk your teacher into a **bonus point** for submitting your paper early—just to make the grading time easier, of course!

- **Now, add to your calendar any other major dates** that may interfere with or interrupt your work or schedule during this time—so that at a glance, you can clearly identify the open time you have to work on this assignment. Add a copy of this "revised" calendar to your notebook. Challenge yourself to stay ahead of schedule.

Step 2: Follow this "WORK SMART" checklist.

_____ **Create a niche**—a quiet, comfortable work space large enough to keep all your work "stuff" together: research material, style manual, dictionary, thesaurus, reference books, due date calendar, alarm clock or kitchen timer, computer and printer, space for snacks and such.

_____ **Place cell phones and other communication or entertainment devices outside of the working area** so that you are not tempted to use them, and so that you at least have to get up to stretch your legs and free your mind when they ring, chime, buzz, chirp, or sing. Limit your conversations by setting a timer (no more than five minutes) when you begin talking.

_____ **Choose a buddy to whom you can brag or whine when needed.** Keep a noisemaker nearby for celebrating small successes, and a pillow or punching bag for releasing frustration. It's also a good idea to have a twisty or rubbery toy to spin, squeeze, or mash while you're thinking.

_____ **As you work, you may wish to keep a supply of healthy munchies available.** (Beware of those that are very starchy or sugary; they will make you sleepy!)

_____ **Get up at least every 30 minutes to stretch and walk or run in place.** You might even take a quick sprint around the block—but nothing strenuous enough to make your body beg for a nap.

Step 3: Take out an insurance policy.

Identify at least three people who are knowledgeable about writing and research papers. Good choices are: English teachers, school or public librarians, neighbors, parents, older siblings, classmates—anyone who loves grammar and writing. Make a copy of your paper for each reader and keep track by checking the appropriate spaces when papers are given and returned. To ensure that your paper is as perfect as possible, schedule an appointment with each of them to read your paper critically and make comments, corrections, and suggestions. Make a schedule like the one shown on the "My Research Paper Insurance Policy" graphic organizer. Be sure these review dates are several days earlier than your already early due dates! (See page 101 in this book.)

My Research Paper Insurance Policy

My name: _____

Paper topic or title:_____

Rough Draft

Name of Reader	Appointment Day and Time	Paper Delivered to Reader	Paper Returned by Reader

Final Draft

Name of Reader	Appointment Day and Time	Paper Delivered to Reader	Paper Returned by Reader

You may use a different set of people for the Final Draft, if you wish.

Step 4: Find the sources you need.

- Ask yourself, "What kinds of sources do I need?"

... encyclopedias (general information)   ... websites

... periodicals, journals, and newspapers   ... blogs

... media presentations   ... maps or atlases

... biographical reference   ... interviews

... audio or visual recordings   ... books

- Ask your librarians to help you locate the best resources for your topic.
- Choose reliable sources. Use websites that are current, clearly show who is responsible for the site, and belong to credible organizations.

Preview the Sources

- Skim the table of contents, index, headings, and opening and closing paragraphs to see if you can find material related to your topic.
- Check out a book's preface or any summaries of resources to see if the source includes the same topics you are seeking or answers the same questions you are pursuing.
- Take a quick look at any illustrations, charts, graphs, video clips, etc., that might reveal whether or not the source is going to be helpful.
- Do your best to find out if the source is reliable for the kind of information given. (See Chapter 7 in this book.)
- If the source looks promising, read bits here and there to see if the information seems useful for your purposes.

BRIGHT IDEA!

Keep a record of all sources you use. (Follow your style guide.) Take notes or copy portions of pages you may use. Get all the information when you first use the source. You don't want to have to go back and track it down. Keep these pages in a notebook until your final paper is returned to you. Record all works cited on notebook pages or index cards (one source to a card) to be stored in the same notebook or in an electronic text file. Number the sources. This will make things **much** easier later!

Step 5: Take notes and write small portions.

Use a spiral notebook so you won't lose any pages. (Choose one that has been three-hole punched so you can add it to your notebook.) Or, take notes on a computer or tablet. Be sure to keep a backup copy.

- Look for central ideas related to your topic. Find several credible and relevant details, facts, or examples to support each idea.

- As you read and take notes, be sure you have a way to tell the difference between the author's words and your own words. If you use words or phrases from the source, put them in quotation marks and note the source and page number(s) in parentheses.

BRIGHT IDEA!

The easiest way to avoid plagiarism is to read the author's words and immediately translate those thoughts into your own words and write them (so that you don't have to worry later about which is which). Save time and confusion later by summarizing or paraphrasing right now the material you plan to use!

- If you use **any** language from your sources in your final draft **without** quote marks **and** the correct documentation, you are guilty of plagiarism. It is easy to make this mistake, but still it is a serious offense. Mixing your own words with the author's words without putting quote marks around the words you have borrowed is a huge academic NO-NO! (You may borrow the author's meaning, but not his or her exact words!)

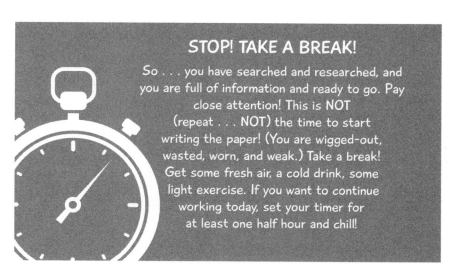

STOP! TAKE A BREAK!

So . . . you have searched and researched, and you are full of information and ready to go. Pay close attention! This is NOT (repeat . . . NOT) the time to start writing the paper! (You are wigged-out, wasted, worn, and weak.) Take a break! Get some fresh air, a cold drink, some light exercise. If you want to continue working today, set your timer for at least one half hour and chill!

Step 6: Create a thesis statement.

- When you have gathered your sources and reread all your notes, it is time to write a sentence that communicates to the reader the one most important piece of information, conclusion, or idea that you want understood.

- This is a statement that you will support with many pieces of evidence (convincing points and paragraphs). *Your whole paper hinges heavily on this statement.*

- When you are satisfied that you have a good thesis, look through your notes to make sure that you have plenty of evidence to support it. If you don't, you will either need to find more evidence or craft a thesis that you can support.

Example of Good Thesis Statement

TOPIC: Using grades as assessment of achievement in middle school studies

THESIS: *A single squiggle on paper cannot begin to tell the story of a middle school student's six-week or six-month journey in learning.*

Step 7: Make a preliminary outline.

- Review your notes to find the parts or ideas that you can use to support, prove, or verify your thesis statement. (You should be able to use these ideas to develop at least five major paragraphs—enough to convince the reader that what you have said in your thesis statement is worthy and true.)

- List these ideas in a rough outline form (then, a formal outline, if required). Read the outline back to yourself to see if your ideas and your source materials actually can produce as much convincing information as you need to write those major paragraphs. If not, return to your resources and hunt for additional points to support your thesis. (Add them to your outline.)

BRIGHT IDEA!

Document your sources in a consistent manner **as you write your rough draft.** This will save you much time and worry later. As you summarize or paraphrase a source in your writing, document it using the required style system. (Keep your MLA, APA, or other required style guide handy at all times.) This will greatly simplify creating your Works Cited page when you have completed your paper.

STOP! TAKE A BREAK!

Now you are ready to roll! Take a deep breath—and raid the fridge for some protein and a refreshing drink. Set timer for 10–20 minutes.

Step 8: Write a draft.

This is your ROUGH draft! Don't worry about perfect grammar, sentence structure, and vocabulary. Just get those ideas down on paper. Write in your own "voice" (language you are comfortable with) and write what you believe about your subject in a way that will convince your reader. Use your outline, your own voice, and try to avoid the language of the sources, except for direct quotes, of course. When you are satisfied that you have said **what** you want to say, reread your work aloud to catch mistakes and perfect your language so that you are happy with **how well** you have said it.

A. Write the introduction.

The introduction should be entirely your own words (unless you open with a short quote to which you refer later in the first paragraph). One paragraph should be enough to grab your reader's attention and introduce your ideas.

Put your thesis statement near the beginning or the end of your introductory paragraph—whichever placement you think will more powerfully affect the readers. In addition to stating the thesis, come up with an extraordinary sentence that will "hook" your reader into this big, main idea.

STOP! TAKE A BREAK!

Take a 10-minute break! Do something active! Set your timer!

B. Write the body of the paper.

This is your opportunity to expand and explain each of the major ideas or points that supports your thesis statement.

- Each new idea should be expressed in a new paragraph.

- You may use as few as five long paragraphs or as many as 12, depending upon how much supportive material you have and the required length of the paper.

- Introduce ideas in an order that will make most sense to the reader.

- Develop each point using clear and appropriate diction (word choice).

- You may be tired of hearing this, but it can't be emphasized enough: support each main idea adequately with reliable, memorable details, facts, or examples.

BRIGHT IDEA!

Enter sources for each idea as you progress so you won't have to retrace steps to locate them later. To avoid plagiarism as you write, review your source statements, then cover them and restate them **in your own words**. Use a thesaurus to locate alternative words as you need them. **Don't keep looking back** at the author's words.

STOP! TAKE A BREAK!

This could probably be an overnight break, unless of course, you are one of those procrastinators whose paper is due in the morning. In that case, run in place for five minutes or take a 15-minute walk. This also might be a time to have a healthy snack and a hydrating drink. Then GET BUSY!

C. Rough out the conclusion.

Congratulations! The end is in sight (well, just over the hill a bit). You have been reading, writing, and thinking for days! (Weeks?) You may be tired of this project and feeling ornery. HOWEVER, before you stop, do yourself a favor! While all the above ideas are fresh in your mind, ask yourself this question: "What is the main idea I want my reader to understand and believe?" Take a minute or two to write the answer to that question quickly, in your own words, on scrap paper. Don't stop to perfect it—just get it down. Check back with your introduction to be sure the conclusion connects to what you started out to prove.

STOP! TAKE THE LAST BREAK!

Eat, dance, laugh, celebrate that you are almost through this long ordeal.
Set your timer for at least 25 minutes.

D. Write the conclusion.

Come back to your niche refreshed and ready to perform your final magic—transforming your fast and messy conclusion into a brilliantly written paragraph that wraps up and ties a bow on what this whole paper has tried to say to the reader! To do that, you must restate in different words the big ideas that you proposed in your introduction **and** add something fresh and new and brilliant to stun your reader into amazement and agreement. Make it so convincing and captivating that, after having finished the last word, the reader is likely to holler, "WOW! Wish I'd written that!"

Step 9: Document sources with a "Works Cited" page.

- Sit down in a quiet place with your almost-finished paper, your list of resources, and your style manual. Read through your paper, one paragraph at a time, carefully noting places where you have used words (and paraphrases of words) that are not wholly your own. Be sure that at the end of those sentences or paragraphs, you have given full and correct credit to the author or source. Don't allow yourself to get lazy and become a plagiarist!

- As you check these in-text citations, you should also create your final list of resources to include on your **Works Cited** page. By the time you finish your Works Cited page, you will have only **one single entry** for each source you have mentioned in your in-text citations, no matter how many quotes or references you have made to that source.

- Don't hesitate to ask for help from your teacher or a librarian with your "Works Cited" page if you are confused. This can seem complicated!

- Next, get away from your paper (for a whole day, if possible).

Step 10: Proofread, polish, and turn in your paper.

- When your mind and body have had a rest, print a copy of your paper; then, with a colored pen in hand, read the entire paper **aloud** to yourself, editing as you go. Immediately, return to your niche and make all corrections.

- When you are satisfied that your paper is ready for the critics, make copies to give to your three readers.

- As your readers return the papers, take time to consider each suggestion and each comment carefully; then make the necessary changes.

- When you are satisfied that your paper is complete, sit down and read it **aloud** to yourself one more time. This is likely to ensure that you will catch any new errors and discover any problems—such as having deleted something by mistake.

ICING ON THE CAKE

- Turn your paper in at the earliest possible opportunity—possibly, well before the deadline.

- Congratulate yourself on a job well done with honesty, accuracy, exceptional readability, and a touch of flair!

- Treat yourself to a favorite activity.

- And, oh—send off a quick email, note, or small gift to thank each reader and any other person who offered special help on your paper.

HELPFUL TIPS

TIP #1 INTRODUCING DIRECT QUOTES *(telling exactly what a person said)*

Dr. Shrink, well-known psychiatrist of the 1960s, writes, " _____ ."

Powerful executive of Doggies Anonymous, Bruce Barker, insists " _____ ."

In a recent *NY Times* article, Hosea Juarez announced, " _____ ."

President Teddy Roosevelt is remembered for yelling, " _____ ."

In her book, _____ , author Kay Knowitall says, " _____ ."

TIP #2 EXPLAINING QUOTES *(using your own words to tell what someone has said)*

Dr. Pencil's point is that _____ .

In other words, Papa Bear is demonstrating that _____ .

Basically, Barker is arguing that _____ .

Obviously, the Secretary of State believes _____ .

TIP #3 INTRODUCING WHAT OTHERS HAVE SAID *(without quoting or explaining them)*

The National Society of Disgruntled Parents issued harsh criticism toward children's author Dr. Seuss for his excessive rhyming.

In a recent political TV news program, both Republicans and Democrats criticized Barnum and Bailey circus clowns for making fun of their political parties.

Most of the middle school students polled agreed that Christmas and spring breaks are not long enough.

TIP #4 INTRODUCING GENERAL VIEWS AND OPINIONS

Many people believe that _____ .

The American government generally takes the position that _____ .

This issue is critically regarded by news broadcasters as _____ .

The public's normal response to this assumption is that _____ .

It is often assumed that _____ .

On this issue, public opinion dictates that _____ .

Most teenagers would argue that _____ .

TIP #5 ADDING INTERPRETATION (in your own words)

What is important here is _____

Given the facts, I would conclude _____

What _____ means to say is _____

Essentially, I am convinced that _____

In the final analysis, it seems _____

To restate it differently, _____

From a different point of view, _____

Given my experience, I believe _____

As a result of recent research, _____

One could also interpret that _____

TIP #6 VERBS TO INTRODUCE SIGNAL PHRASES (In place of "_____ says, . . .")

adds	contends	insists	rejects
affirms	declares	maintains	remarks
agrees	denies	mentions	reports
alleges	discloses	notes	responds
answers	disputes	offers	sides with
argues	emphasizes	pleads	suggests
asserts	establishes	points out	suspects
believes	estimates	questions	testifies
claims	implies	recognizes	thinks
confirms	indicates	reiterates	verbalizes

TIP #7 A TREASURY OF TRANSITIONAL WORDS AND PHRASES

accordingly	conversely	in the same way	regardless
actually	even so	incidentally	similarly
admittedly	finally	instead	specifically
after all	for example	likewise	still
all together	furthermore	meanwhile	subsequently
as a matter of fact	hence	moreover	then
as a result	however	naturally	therefore
at any rate	in addition	nevertheless	thus
at the same time	in conclusion	next	to be sure
besides	in fact	of course	to put it bluntly
certainly	in other words	on the contrary	ultimately
consequently	in short	otherwise	yet

Chapter 9

Captivate Every Learner with Authentic Learning

*Integrating Multiple Intelligences and Thinking Skills
with Student-Centered Lessons and Projects*

by Sandra Schurr

Original Curriculum Project Planner by Imogene Forte and Sandra Schurr

Teaching Different Learners

Authentic learning occurs when classroom experiences
- fit the thinking and learning styles of the learners
- involve students in using their minds well
- build, stretch, and challenge thinking skills
- translate to meaningful products and performances, in and out of school
- are assessed in ways that extend the learning

This chapter shows how three major instructional models interface with one another for designing high-quality lesson plans, project plans, interdisciplinary units, learning tasks, and assessment tasks that are the base for authentic learning experiences. This guide gives student actions, products, presentations, sample learning tasks, and assessment options—all keyed to Howard Gardner's Multiple Intelligences, Benjamin Bloom's Levels of Higher Cognitive Development, and Williams' Levels of Creative Thinking. (See pages 111-115.)

The "Linking Learning" suggestions on pages 116-125 are organized under the nine multiple-intelligence categories and linked to levels of cognitive development (Bloom) and levels of creative thinking (Williams). Combine actions and behaviors with suggested products or performances for learning adventures to fit natural intelligence and learning-style tendencies. Then choose an assessment format that fits the learner! (Use the graphic organizer on page 126 to plan lessons or units.)

Every category of suggestions is ripe with possibilities for another kind of integration—connecting learning processes to technology. Watch for opportunities for students to use computers, smart devices, and any other technological gadgets available as they brainstorm, research, create, experiment, produce, share, and give feedback on their learning adventures. (See pages 8 through 11 for technology-connection ideas for language arts learning.)

Gardner's Multiple Intelligences

Howard Gardner argues that students learn in ways that are distinctive from individual to individual. Thus, individuals need access to differing approaches, materials, processes, products, and assessments to learn in effective ways. The categories below are not rigid. Each individual has a unique combination of ways to interact with and learn from the world.

LINGUISTIC INTELLIGENCE (Word Smart)

FOCUS: the power of the spoken and written word; the acts of reading, writing, listening, and speaking

To identify: Watch for those who have well-developed verbal skills and sensitivity to the sounds, meanings, and rhythms of words; who have excellent auditory receptive (input) and verbal expressive (output) skills; and who like to read, write, play word and card games, solve word puzzles, listen to recordings or speeches, discuss and converse, take notes and keep journals, or speak out on a subject or topic.

LOGICAL-MATHEMATICAL INTELLIGENCE (Number Smart)

FOCUS: the abilities to engage in scientific thinking and inductive/deductive reasoning, interpret data, analyze abstract patterns, see relationships, and solve problems

To identify: Watch for those who are able to think conceptually and abstractly; identify numeric patterns; speak with a "reasoned voice"; and who like to: perform calculations, play number and logic games, work with computer spreadsheets and databases, conduct science investigations, engage in cause-and-effect thinking, analyze and solve problems, solve brainteasers, or construct graphs and timelines.

VISUAL-SPATIAL INTELLIGENCE (Art Smart)

FOCUS: eye-hand coordination; the ability to create and manipulate mental images in the visual world; the orientation of the body in space and of objects or places

To identify: Watch for those who think and process information through pictures and images; who have excellent visual receptive skills, fine motor skills, vivid imaginations, and an unusual ability to conceptualize the world; and who like to: make maps, blueprints, or floor plans; do jigsaw puzzles and solve mazes; build things; develop videos or movies; create web pages or podcasts; play board games; draw, paint, or sculpt; or design things (such as homes, buildings, furnishings, costumes, fashions, or hairstyles).

BODILY-KINESTHETIC INTELLIGENCE (Body Smart)

FOCUS: the ability to work skillfully with objects involving both fine and gross motor skills; having a strong sense of one's own manual dexterity, physical agility, balance, and eye/hand coordination

To identify: Watch for those who know how to control their body movements and express themselves through physical activities; are highly aware of the world through touch and movement; and who like to: play outdoor games and sports, perform dances, play charades or work puppets, act out scenes from plays or movies, play with blocks and other construction materials, do arts and crafts, or work with hands-on tools and equipment.

MUSICAL INTELLIGENCE (Music Smart)

FOCUS: auditory skills; the way one can hear tones, rhythms, and musical patterns through the human voice and as part of the environment; an individual's ability to understand and express oneself through music and rhythmic movements

To identify: Watch for those who show the ability to understand the relationship between sound and feeling; who think, feel, and process information primarily through music; and who like to: listen to music, play an instrument, dance, drum, review sheet music, sing in a choir, create raps or poems, chant, or make up advertising jingles and commercials.

INTERPERSONAL INTELLIGENCE (People Smart)

FOCUS: the ability to get along well with others; the individual skills of being able to collaborate, socialize, compromise, interact, and care for those with whom one comes into contact

To identify: Watch for those who have the capacity to detect and respond appropriately to the moods, motivations, and desires of others and who like to: do group projects, take part in debates and panels, role-play, conduct interviews or surveys, tutor or coach others, play games, enjoy text or instant messaging, or join online chat rooms.

INTRAPERSONAL INTELLIGENCE (Self Smart)

FOCUS: the ability to recognize and accept his/her own strengths and weaknesses; an individual's natural intuition and inner wisdom

To identify: Watch for those who have a capacity to be self-aware and in-tune with their inner feelings, values, beliefs, and thinking processes; who have a strong sense of independence and self-confidence; and who like to: work and play alone, take part in helping other people, keep personal diaries or journals, undertake activities to learn about themselves, pursue individual hobbies, engage in self-help and self-directed activities, or conduct online or library research.

NATURALIST INTELLIGENCE (Nature Smart)

FOCUS: the ability to navigate easily in the natural world and see the patterns in nature; an understanding and valuing of Earth's ecosystem

To identify: Watch for those who are attuned to nature; who appreciate the intricacies and subtleties of the connectedness found within the environment; and who like to: identify and categorize rocks, plants, or animals; explore and wander outdoors; predict weather based on patterns; build models of varied plants, animals, and landforms; plant and tend gardens; care for pets and animals; or collect and create artwork using items found in nature.

EXISTENTIALIST INTELLIGENCE (Wonder Smart)

FOCUS: the proclivity to pose and ponder questions about life, death, and ultimate realities; thinking about life's big issues

To identify: Look for those who are curious about deep questions of human existence, life, death, and ultimate realities, and who like to: think of questions (sometimes unanswerable) beyond those of most children and adults; study different dimensions of life and death; examine philosophical positions and ideas; work with complex theories; seek information about spiritual and religious ideologies; or look for scientific evidence to validate unnatural events and psychic predictions.

Source: Gardner, H. (1983). *Frames of mind: The theory of multiple intelligences.* New York: Basic Books.

Bloom's Taxonomy of Cognitive Processes

The six levels of thinking begin with the lowest and move to the highest.

REMEMBERING: Retrieving, recognizing, and recalling relevant knowledge from long-term memory (*This level focuses on the act of remembering when memory is used to produce definitions, facts, or lists and on the act of reciting or retrieving material.*)

UNDERSTANDING: Constructing meaning from oral, written, and graphic messages through interpreting, exemplifying, classifying, summarizing, inferring, comparing, and explaining (*This level emphasizes one's ability to understand uses and implications of terms, facts, methods, procedures, and concepts.*)

APPLYING: Carrying out or using a procedure through executing or implementing (*This level refers to new situations where one makes use of learned material through products like models, presentations, interviews, or simulations.*)

ANALYZING: Breaking material or concepts into constituent parts, determining how the parts relate or interrelate to one another or to an overall structure through differentiating, organizing, and attributing (*This level encourages one to analyze structure, recognize assumptions and poor logic, and evaluate relevancy by creating spreadsheets, surveys, charts, diagrams, or other graphic representations.*)

EVALUATING: Making judgments based on criteria and standards through checking and critiquing (*This level involves the act of setting standards, judging or using standards, producing evidence, and accepting or rejecting evidence on the basis of sound criteria through products such as critiques, recommendations, and reports.*)

CREATING: Putting elements together to form a coherent or functional whole; reorganizing elements into a new pattern or structure through generating, planning, or producing (*This level requires users to put parts together in a new way or synthesize parts into something different, resulting in a unique form, original product, functional whole, or such a coherent work as a speech, experiment, essay, or drama.*)

Source: Bloom, B. S.; Engelhart, M. D.; Furst, E. J.; Hill, W. H.; & Krathwohl, D. R. (1956). *Taxonomy of educational objectives: The classification of educational goals. Handbook I: Cognitive domain.* New York: David McKay Company.

NOTE: *Bloom's Taxonomy is also a two-dimensional model that identifies and describes the various forms of knowledge: factual, conceptual, procedural, and metacognitive.*

Williams' Taxonomy of Creative Thinking

The eight levels should be taught by educators in a logical sequence from fluency to imagination.

FLUENCY enables the learner to generate a great many ideas, related answers, or choices in a given situation. (Cue words: *generating lots, many, oodles of ideas*)

FLEXIBILITY lets the learner change everyday objects to generate a variety of categories by taking detours and varying sizes, shapes, quantities, time limits, requirements, objectives, or dimensions in a given situation. (Cue words: *generating varied, different, alternative ideas*)

ORIGINALITY causes the learner to seek new ideas by suggesting unusual twists to change content or inventing clever responses to a given situation. (Cue words: *generating unusual, unique, new ideas*)

ELABORATION helps the learner stretch by expanding, enlarging, enriching, or embellishing possibilities that build on previous thoughts or ideas. (Cue words: *generating enriched, embellished, elaborative, or expanded ideas*)

RISK TAKING enables the learner to deal with the unknown by taking chances, experimenting with new ideas, or trying new challenges. (Cue words: *experimenting with and exploring risky ideas*)

COMPLEXITY permits the learner to create structure in an unstructured setting or build a logical order in a given situation. (Cue words: *improving and explaining ideas*)

CURIOSITY encourages the learner to follow a hunch, question alternatives, ponder outcomes, and wonder about options in a given situation. (Cue words: *pondering and questioning ideas*)

IMAGINATION allows the learner to visualize possibilities, build images in his or her mind, picture new objects, or reach beyond the limits of the practical. (Cue words: *visualizing and fantasizing ideas*)

Source: Williams, F. E. (1970). *Classroom ideas for encouraging thinking and feeling.* Buffalo, N.Y.: D.O.K. Publishers.

Linking Learning : LINGUISTIC INTELLIGENCE

Action Verbs and Student Behaviors

Adapt	Define	Form	Name	Recite	Stretch
Answer	Describe	Generalize	Paraphrase	Recommend	Suggest
Argue	Discuss	Generate	Predict	Relate	Summarize
Associate	Elaborate	Indicate	Prescribe	Repeat	Suppose
Clarify	Embellish	Interpret	Present	Rephrase	Synthesize
Convince	Enrich	Interview	Question	Restate	Teach
Critique	Explain	List	Quote	Retell	Tell
Debate	Express	Memorize	Read	Rewrite	Translate
Defend	Extend	Modify	Recall	Specify	Write

Suggested Student Products and Performances

Advertisements	Digital presentations	Literature circles	Riddles
Audio recordings	Dramatic readings	Logs	Sequels
Blogs	Emails	Movies	Similes
Choral readings	Essays	Multimedia projects	Speeches
Class newspapers	Explanations	Online articles	Storytelling
Comedy acts	Flash cards	Pamphlets	Summaries
Conversations	Grammar diagrams	Plays	Teach a lesson
Creative writing	How-to guides	Podcasts	Translate to another
Crossword puzzles	Impromptu speeches	Poems	language
Debates	Instructions	Posters	Tweets
Descriptions	Interviews	Puppet shows	Web pages
Dialogues	Journals	Reader's theater	Word games
Diaries	Letters	Reports	Word problems

Optional Assessment Formats

Agree or disagree statements	Discussion points	Kinesthetic tests	Rough or final drafts
Anecdotal records	Essays	Linguistic humor	Rubrics
Audio recordings	Formal speeches	Portfolios	Starter statements
Checklists	Game show-style tests	Quizzes	Summaries
Debates	Graphic organizers	Quotation reactions	"Who Am I?" or
		Reflection logs	"What Am I?" games

Sample Learning Tasks:

Math: Orally explain two different strategies that could be used to solve a particular math problem.

Science: Write a poem to teach the meaning of a "big" science idea, such as equilibrium or cause and effect.

Health and P.E.: Write a script for a video to demonstrate a first-aid technique.

Linking Learning: LOGICAL-MATHEMATICAL INTELLIGENCE

Action Verbs and Student Behaviors

Account for	Conclude	Find	Model	Reverse
Adapt	Contrast	relationships	Modify	Sequence
Analyze	Convert	Find unknowns	Observe	Simplify
Apply	Diagram	Formulate	Order	Solve
Brainstorm	Differentiate	Hypothesize	Organize	Strategize
Calculate	Estimate	Infer	Outline	Track
Categorize	Evaluate	Integrate	Predict	Translate
Clarify	Explain	Interpret	Prove	Verify
Classify	Extrapolate	Justify	Rank	Wonder
Compare	Find examples	Measure	Record	Work backwards

Suggested Student Products and Performances

Analyses (oral, visual, or written)	Coded messages	Matrices	Story grids
Attribute puzzles	Data collections	Mind maps	Summaries
Calculations	Deductive reasoning	Outlines	Syllogisms
Calculator games	Diagrams	Patterns	Teach a lesson
Cause-effect explanations	Graphic organizers	Predictions	Time sequence charts
Challenge tasks	Graphs or tables	Problem construction	Timelines
Charts	Inductive reasoning	Science experiments	Webs
Classification displays	Logic games or puzzles	Science fair projects	Word problems
		Sequences	

Optional Assessment Formats

Arguments	Graphic organizers	Restating problems
Bloom-based tests	How-to recipes	Rubrics
Charts	Identify strategies	Simplifications
Checklists	Inductive reasoning tasks	Strategy explanations
Critiques	Inquiry explanations	Summaries
Deductive reasoning tasks	Logic exercises	Translations (word problems into equations)
Diagrams	Outlines	
Estimate solutions	Pattern games	Verbal explanations
Experiment logs	Problem-solving diagrams	Verify solutions
Fix wrong answers	"Read and Explain" challenges	Webs
Formula explanations		"What if" exercises

Sample Learning Tasks:

Fine Arts: Create a visual design with numbers and mathematical symbols.

Language Arts: Chart the structure of sentences in a particular essay.

History: Rank 10 historical events in terms of the importance of their lasting influence.

Linking Learning: VISUAL-SPATIAL INTELLIGENCE

Action Verbs and Student Behaviors

Arrange	Demonstrate	Envision	Improve	Observe	Represent
Augment	Design	Expand	Integrate	Organize	Reproduce
Build	Diagram	Form	Interpret	Outline	Show
Change	Draw	Graph	Invent	Produce	Stretch
Compose	Dream	Identify	Label	Rearrange	Transform
Convert	Embellish	Illustrate	List	Recognize	Visualize
Create	Enlarge	Imagine	Model	Reorder	Wonder

Suggested Student Products and Performances

Animation	Exhibits	Movies	Relief maps or
Book covers	Experiments	Murals	exhibits
Charts	Flow charts	Paintings	Role playing
Chess games	Graphic organizers	Pamphlets	Stage design
Codes	Graphs	Personal web pages	Theatrics
Collages	Illustrations	Photographs	Time machines
Comic strips	Images	Picture dictionaries	Use of manipulatives
Computer graphics	Maps	Podcasts	Venn diagrams
Designs	Mind maps	Postcards	Video clips
Diagrams	Mobiles	Posters	Webs
Drawings	Models	Puzzles	Web page designs

Optional Assessment Formats

Demonstrations	Lists	Picture or symbol cards
Designs	Maps	Portfolios
Diagrams	Models	Puzzles
Drawings	Montages	Response cards
Flow charts	Murals	Rubrics
Graphic organizers	Observation logs	Scrapbooks
Graphs	Photo albums	Video presentations
Illustrations	Photo essays	Visual pattern completions
Learning posters	Picture books	Webs

Sample Learning Tasks:

Culture and Geography: Rename Earth's large bodies of water, based on each one's visual appearance.

Language Arts: Visually organize ideas for a speech in the form of a map or web.

Science: Draw molecules to depict the chemical components of compounds.

Linking Learning: BODILY-KINESTHETIC INTELLIGENCE

Action Verbs and Student Behaviors

Acquire	Construct	Feel	Match	Prepare	Show
Act out	Count	Find	Measure	Present	Simulate
Adjust	Create	Fold	Model	Produce	Sort
Arrange	Dance	Form	Modify	Rearrange	Spin
Bend	Demonstrate	Group	Move	Reconstruct	Stretch
Blend	Design	Imitate	Operate	Reorder	Survey
Build	Develop	Inspect	Order	Reorganize	Touch
Change	Devise	Interpret	Organize	Role-play	Trace
Classify	Discover	Invent	Pantomime	Rotate	Track
Collect	Dramatize	Investigate	Perform	Search	Transfer
Combine	Examine	Jump	Plan	Select	Twist
Complete	Execute	Locate	Point	Separate	Uncover
Conduct	Experiment	Manipulate	Practice	Shake	Write

Suggested Student Products and Performances

Acting	Facial expressions	Projects	Sports
Body formations	Games	Reenactments	Staging
Charades	Gestures	Role playing	Theatrics
Collections	Impersonations	Routines	Touch, smell, feel,
Costumes	Interviews	(gymnastic)	listen activities
Dances	Inventions	Sculpture	Use of manipulatives
Demonstrations	Keyboarding	Sign language	Use of textures
Dramas	Martial arts	Simulations	Video productions
Exercises	Mimes	Skits	
Experiments	Pantomimes	"Spell" aerobics	

Optional Assessment Formats

Charades	Impersonations	Portfolios
Checklists	Interpretations	Role playing
Demonstrations	Kinesthetic tests	Simulations
Dramatizations	Mimes	Speeches
Exercise routines	Movement games	Use of manipulatives
Games	Performances	

Sample Learning Tasks:

Science: Place different kinds of soil in paper bags. Identify the soils by feeling them, without looking.

Fine Arts: Use body gestures to show responses to different kinds of music.

Math: Use body motions to demonstrate adjacent (or other) angles.

Linking Learning: MUSICAL INTELLIGENCE

Action Verbs and Student Behaviors

Amplify	Conduct	Express	Interpret	Play	Respond
Arrange	Contrast	Harmonize	Invent	Practice	Retell
Associate	Create	Hear	Lip sync	Present	Select
Chant	Dance	Hum	Listen	Rap	Show
Classify	Demonstrate	Illustrate	Modify	Recognize	Sing
Collaborate	Drum	Imagine	Move	Record	Syncopate
Compare	Enhance	Improvise	Pattern	Reflect on	Vocalize
Compose	Evaluate	Incorporate	Perform	Represent	Write about

Suggested Student Products and Performances

Chants	Interpretative dances	Playing instruments
Cheers	Jingles	Podcasts with music
Choral presentations	Jump-rope rhymes	Poems
Choral readings	Match concepts to	Radio or TV shows
Compare or contrast music	music	Raps
or rhythms	Match text to music	Rhythm games
Compositions	Melodies	Rhythmic patterns
Create electronic music	Morse code	Set concepts to rhythm or
Cross-cultural music	Move to rhythm	music
Design musical instruments	Music notation	Show scripts
Dialogues	Musical interpretations	Songs
Humming	Musical plays	Sound effects
Identify instruments	Physical performances to	Video productions
Identify sounds	music	Web pages with sound

Optional Assessment Formats

Analysis of music structure	Dances	Original songs or raps
Comparisons or contrasts	Mnemonics involving rhythm	Pattern completions
Concepts or facts set	Music arrangements	Poetry
to music	Musical collages	Reproducing tone patterns
Concepts or facts set to	Musical compositions	Rubrics
rhythms	Musical interpretations	

Sample Learning Tasks for Musical Intelligence

Language Arts: Sing the definitions of vocabulary words set to familiar, simple tunes.

History: Construct a musical timeline of a country's history.

Culture and Geography: Listen to rhythmic selections from different cultures and identify each culture's unique features.

Linking Learning: INTERPERSONAL INTELLIGENCE

Action Verbs and Student Behaviors

Advise	Critique	Experience	Organize	Respond
Argue	Debate	Explain	Plan	Role-play
Associate	Decide	Give feedback	Practice	Seek
Brainstorm	Demonstrate	Improve	Present	Share
Coach	Design	Infer	Question	Show
Collaborate	Discuss	Interview	Receive feed-	Solve
Communicate	Empathize	Justify	back	Support
Connect	Encounter	Listen	Record	Talk
Co-create	Evaluate	Motivate	Relate	Teach

Suggested Student Products and Performances

Assembly lines	Emails	Partnerships
Biographies	Empathy practices	Peer coaching
Blogs	Give and receive feedback	Podcasts
Circles of knowledge	Group problem-solving	Role-playing
Co-author projects	Group web pages	Simulations
Communication games	Human graphs	Surveys
Comparisons or contrasts	Inside-outside circles	Team learning
Conflict resolution	Instant messages	Think, pair, and share
Cooperative projects	Interviews	Translate observations or
Dialogues	Joint presentations	feelings
Discussions	Letters	Trust games
"Each one teach one"	Literature circles	Video "letters"

Optional Assessment Formats

Buzz sessions	Group inquiries	Rubrics
Collaborative tests	Group problem-solving tasks	Scavenger hunts
Concentration game	Group puzzles	Test, coach, retest
Debates	Partner quizzes	Think, pair, and share
Group fact-finding	Project posters	Tic-Tac-Toe
Group goal evaluations	Round-robin responses	

Sample Learning Tasks:

History: Plan and stage mock trials for famous villains in history.

Math: Compare your solution to a problem with someone who solved the same problem in a different way.

Culture and Geography: Conduct a survey to find locations where class members have lived or traveled.

Linking Learning: INTRAPERSONAL INTELLIGENCE

Action Verbs and Student Behaviors

Access	Contrast	Explain	List	Rewrite
Analyze	Create	Explore	Plan	Select
Appraise	Critique	Express	Practice	Self-reflect
Appreciate	Decide	Focus	Process	Share
Assess	Defend	Illustrate	Propose	Show
Assimilate	Describe	Imagine	Rank	Support
Award	Determine	Interpolate	Rate	Tell
Compare	Discriminate	Interpret	Recognize	Track
Concentrate	Draw	Invent	Reflect	Validate
Conclude	Evaluate	Judge	Revise	Write

Suggested Student Products and Performances

Autobiographies	Intuition logs	Personal correlations to
Brain-training exercises	Journals	history
Career goals	Learning logs	Personal priorities
Concentration skills	Metacognitive surveys	Photo essays
Diaries	Mnemonics	Poetry
Goal setting	Monologues	Point-of-view collections
Guided imagery	Observations	Reflections
Hero stories	Opinion-share	Self-reflections
Identify learning style	Personal action plans	Self-surveys
Impersonations		Share opinions

Optional Assessment Formats

Anecdotal card files	Individual conferences	Project posters
Anecdotal records	Individual goal evaluations	Reflections
Bloom-based tests	Journals and logs	Rubrics
Checklists	Metacognitive inquiries	Self-inventories
Diaries	Portfolios	Self-progress reports
Independent contracts	Position statements	Self-quizzes

Sample Learning Tasks:

Health and P.E.: Design a personal month-long fitness plan.

Language Arts: Select a poem that expresses an idea the way you would have expressed it. Add a stanza.

Math: Generate a math conundrum that relates to your real life.

Linking Learning: NATURALIST INTELLIGENCE

Action Verbs and Student Behaviors

Adapt	Conserve	Experience	Listen	Pursue	Solve
Calculate	Construct	Explain	Manipulate	Reflect	Tame
Care for	Describe	Graph	Nurture	Research	Taste
Classify	Display	Grow	Observe	Sense	Transfer
Collect	Draw	Incorporate	Photograph	Sketch	Write
Compose	Experiment	Interact	Prepare	Smell	

Suggested Student Products and Performances

Adopt-a-highway (or park or pet)
Caring for animals
Catch (and release) butterflies or insects
Categorize rocks or shells
Charts and graphs
Classifications of living things
Collections (seeds, etc.)
Conservation projects
Create nature trails
Displays and models
Experiments
Explanations (natural phenomena)

Field notes
Guides to fishing or hiking
Interviews (with scientists)
Laboratory tasks
Match natural processes to music
Microscopic slides
Nature collages or montages
Nature observations or encounters
Nature-oriented podcasts and blogs
Nature simulations
Organic and inorganic displays
Paintings

Photo essays
Plan organic gardens or parks
Posters
Recording of natural sounds
Recycling plans
Simulations of natural things or phenomena
Stargazing
Storm watching
Taste tests
Video shows
Weather charts
Weather forecasts
Web page design

Optional Assessment Formats

Annotated bibliographies of nature-oriented websites
Applications of deductive reasoning
Applications of inductive reasoning
Case studies of endangered species
Collaborative tests
Data collections

Dramatic enactments
Environmental checklists
Equipment demonstrations
Field notebooks
Forecasts
Graphs of environmental influences
Journal entries
Learning logs

Nature-oriented position papers
Nature-related scrapbooks
Outdoor classroom observations
Photograph albums
Quizzes
Reflections on environmental or scientific issues

Sample Learning Tasks:

Math: Create a directory of mathematical patterns found in nature.

Fine Arts: Invent a musical tune to match the movements of a plant, animal, or water source.

Health and P.E.: Use rocks to build an outdoor obstacle or exercise course.

Linking Learning: EXISTENTIALIST INTELLIGENCE

Action Verbs and Student Behaviors

Argue	Connect	Explore	Question
Ask	Consider	Hypothesize	Reenact
Challenge	Console	Imagine	Reflect
Clarify	Dispute	Inquire	Stretch
Commit	Dramatize	Interpret	Suspend disbelief
Comply	Dream	Ponder	Theorize
Compose	Endorse	Pose	Wonder
Conceptualize	Examine	Preach	

Suggested Student Products and Performances

Biographies of thinkers	Hypotheses	Reviews of philosophical or spiritual systems
Book reviews	Imagination logs	Role-playing
Comparisons and contrasts of ideas	Interpretations	Skits
Diaries	Journals	Soliloquies
Dramas	Pageants	Tableaus
Dramatic readings	Philosophy glossaries	Testimonials
Drawings or diagrams	Plays	Theater-in-the-round
Enactments (spiritual or philosophical ideas)	Poetry	Theories and theory explanations
Essays	Poetry readings	Tributes
	Questions	
	Readers' theater	

Optional Assessment Formats

Analytic essays	Paraphrase of big questions
Comparison of possible answers	Poetry
Contrasting viewpoints	Position statements
Data or evidence collections	Reflections
Graphic organizer of big idea or questions	"So What?" lists
Implications of various positions	Translations to other modes (music, movement, art)
Lists of questions raised	Webs
Outline of questions within the question	

Sample Learning Tasks:

Math: List ideas, concepts, events, or things that could or should continue into infinity.

Health and P.E.: Identify ways that the body might be affected by travel to a different dimension.

Science: Write a list of questions that science cannot answer at this time (and might not ever answer).

Considering It All!
A Plan for Authentic Learning

Lesson or Unit Topic	Intelligences	Cognitive Levels
	Linguistic	Remembering
Introductory Activity	Logical-Mathematical	Understanding
		Analyzing
	Visual	Evaluating
	Bodily-Kinesthetic	Applying
	Musical	Creating
Culminating Activity		
	Interpersonal	**Creativity Levels**
		Fluency
	Intrapersonal	Flexibility
		Originality
	Naturalist	Elaboration
Assessment Options	Existentialist	Risk Taking
		Complexity
		Curiosity
		Imagination

Include in the plan a brief description of a learning activity for each of the intelligences, cognitive skills, and creativity skills.

Name _____ Date_____

Chapter 10

Podcast Your Way to Integrated Learning

*A Step-by-Step Guide for Creating Podcasts
and Using Them in the Classroom*

by Dedra Stafford

Showcasing Language Arts Skills

The term *podcast* is a fusion of the two words *iPod*® and *broadcast*. At its core, a podcast is an audio file that can be downloaded and played on the computer or a portable audio device. *Podcasting* makes digital files available on the Internet. Listeners subscribe to the audio feed and receive new updates automatically. Anyone with an Internet connection and some simple equipment can create a podcast and share it online. A podcast producer plans the podcast, records it using recording and editing software, such as Audacity™ or GarageBand®, uploads it to a podcast distribution portal or website, then creates the RSS feed. (RSS stands for *Really Simple Syndication*. It's what makes an audio recording blossom into a podcast!)

Podcasts are flexible, "anytime" creations that are mostly free. This *anytime* aspect of the podcast is what makes it so popular. Google™, YouTube™, and TiVo® have created a generation of learners that expect an "instant information world." By tapping into this generation's natural interests and skills, teachers can create an engaging learning environment.

A podcast is a splendid way to practice and deepen language arts skills, combine them with technology, and put them to use in a real-life setting. In the processes of consuming and producing podcasts, students apply reading, writing, thinking, listening, and researching skills. In addition, podcasting fosters innovation and creativity. Our study on podcasts concludes this volume because podcasting is a wonderful culminating tool—integrating the important skills students have learned in the other units.

Note: If you are podcasting from school, be sure to check with your school's technology department to ensure that your server can support podcasting. Follow all school procedures for downloading podcasting software and uploading finished podcasts.

Typical "Radio Show" Podcast Format

In creating podcasts, the typical broadcast radio format is a good place to begin because it offers plenty of opportunities for fun, variety, and use of language skills. Students could also choose to create game shows, interviews, or radio dramas, too. But before students create any podcast, have them listen to and critique a few real podcasts to better understand each segment. Students should be careful to never use their full name when participating in a broadcast uploaded to the Internet. Using only first names or creating pseudonyms helps to keep students safe online.

Note: Each segment in a radio show podcast needs a catchy name and possible transitional music between segments.

1. **Introduction music and podcast show announcement**
   "It's the Science Cell Show . . ."

2. **Welcome from the show's host**
   "Welcome, I am your host Regis Phylum!"

3. **"Teaser" (given by the host) of the upcoming segments**
   "Today, we will feature: Live from the Halls with Shawna, the Joke of the Day with T.J., and News Around the World with Tyler."

4. **Intro to each segment and to the speaker for that segment (given by the host for that segment)**
   "Now, let's go to T.J. with the Joke of the Day!"

5. **Closing (given by the show's host; tells the URL of the website where the podcast shows can be found, information about upcoming episodes, and a thanks for listening)**
   "Thanks for listening; don't forget to visit for our website and tune in next week ..."

6. **End with exit music**

Note to the Teacher:

If you want to use podcasting as a way to hook the digital learner, start simply. Record segments of your lessons for a test review, record quick study points for a topic that will be on a test, or record lab steps. As you become comfortable with the process, you can move from teacher-based podcasts to class productions, and eventually, to student or group productions. Podcast creation fosters innovation and creativity as students can plan how to add music and sound effects to the presentations.

Tips for Planning Your Show

Start strong!

Begin your podcast with an opening that grabs your listeners' attention. This should include an introduction to the show and the host. Some podcasts use a catchy song or jingle.

Choose clever segments and dream up catchy names.

"Did You Know?" Trivia Games
Mind Masters of Math!
This Day in History
Mystery-Guest Interview
Class Happenings
Sports Update
News Around the World
Language Tricks and Gimmicks
Brain Busters
Poetry or Creative Writing

Famous Quotes
Hot Spots on the Web for Kids
Shout Outs (Birthdays or Achievements)
Word of the Week or Joke of the Day
Health Tips for Teens
People You Must Know!
Public Service Announcements on such topics
 as Internet Safety or Stamp Out Bullying
Tip of the Day
Believe-It-or-Not Facts

Add sounds!

Use transitional music or sounds to signal each new segment in the show. Create (or find) songs, jingles, segment sounds, and a digital device to play them (iTunes®, Winamp®). Gather gadgets and instruments to create your own sound effects. **Know the legal boundaries for music use.** You must only use music for which you hold the copyright or for which permission is given. You can create your own music or try a search for websites that have podsafe music. Podsafe music is music on the Internet that is available to use free in some cases, or without difficult licensing. The Podsafe Music Network® (PMN), also found as Music Alley®, has a large archive of podsafe music.

Practice good ethics.

Use only public domain or "pod-safe" sounds and music that has been released under a Creative Commons license. Creative Commons licensing means the artist or creator has agreed to allow his or her sounds or music to be used by you in any form or manner for webcasting, as long as you don't take credit for—or make money from—the original work.

End memorably!

As you end your show, promote the next episode with a teaser and then fade out with a piece of exit music.

Step by Step to a Podcast

Step 1 Pre-Production

You will need:

- **A current operating system** — Windows® XP or Mac OS® X

- **A microphone** ($10–$200+) — The more you spend, the better the sound quality; but for most classroom applications, a desktop microphone or a headset with a built-in microphone is a good selection. You can even use the microphone built into your computer, but keep in mind that a built-in microphone may pick up extra noises coming from your computer.

- **Audio-recording software** — Take advantage of a free open-source program, such as Audacity™ (as well as the Lame Encoder plug-in) or GarageBand®. Audacity is cross-platform (can be used with PCs or Macs), easy to use, and, most importantly, free!

- **Web space** — Most schools allow server space for teachers to post webpages. Ideally, this is the place to store your podcasts for others to access them. There are also many sites that allow a certain amount of web space for an inexpensive monthly rate or even for free. To find one of these sites, search the web for "Podcast host or hosting service."

- **Content goals** — The content can be anything! Interviews, audio texts, news events, opinions, lessons, lectures, demonstrations, radio broadcast-type shows, how-to instructions, comedy routines, or quizzes are just a few features that work on podcasts. Before you record, follow these steps to help focus your podcast:

  1. Choose a topic that is focused on your curriculum goals and make sure that there is an educational reason for your podcast.

  2. Decide on the format (e.g., the length, structure, segments, music, and theme song) and the delivery (Who will speak? Is this a teacher production, class production, or small-group production?)

  3. Before recording, write an outline or create a script. Make notes as to places where music or sound effects or other additions to the text should be inserted.

  4. Practice. Find a quiet place with no distractions and take the time to practice your podcast aloud.

Note: Almost every week, a new software program is developed that makes podcast creation simpler and quicker.

Step 2 Production Time: Quiet on the Set

Get ready for your first take: Test your settings and microphone. Tape one segment and then play it back to see if you need to change your settings, microphone, or recording studio for better sound quality. If you are recording at school, remember that bells, announcements, and interruptions can disturb the recording. Create a sign for your door that says, "Recording in progress. Please come back in 15 minutes."

Know that:

- It is best to record in a quiet, secluded room. A microphone can pick up unwanted background noises (people talking, telephone rings, room fans, and machine noise).
- The microphone doesn't have to be right next to your mouth. If the microphone is too close, the recording may be too loud, or your breathing may be heard in the playback. Choose a balanced distance from the microphone.

Record: Follow instructions for the specific recording and editing software you choose. During the recording, try not to stop. *"But what if I make a mistake?"* Keep recording even though you will be tempted to start over. Stay silent for a few seconds (so you can easily identify your mistake later in the edit stage) and then begin again from the point at which you stopped, or from a few lines before the mistake.

Edit and add music: Remove any unwanted parts, noises, and mistakes. When you are happy with the way your recording sounds, it is time to consider adding introductions, transition music, and exit pieces.

Save and convert to MP3: Save the recorded file to your computer in case you choose to do more editing later. Finally, save the project again in MP3 format. MP3 format is the acceptable standard for most podcast recordings.

> *Note: Help students to not get discouraged or frustrated if they dislike what they hear in the playback. Remember, even the best podcasters have to edit and re-record portions to make their project sound great!*

Step 3 Post-Production Time: Welcome to Cyberspace!

To truly become a "podcast," an MP3 needs the RSS feed so that anyone on the Internet can subscribe to and download your episodes. This is where it gets a little dicey for those of us who are not tech experts! Here are two fairly simple ways to create and use an RSS feed:

Option A: Use a "do-it-all" site. Take advantage of some of the complete solution packages that are avaliable online to help you code your files with the needed RSS feed. These websites vary in features and ability but most will host your content in a specific URL, create the RSS feed, allow you to manage your podcast, and list your podcast in their directory. Some of the "do-it-all" sites will give you an audio player to embed into your website, create the iTunes® specs, and submit the podcast to iTunes for you. These sites vary in cost from free to a minimal monthly hosting fee. At the time of publication, *podcastpeople.com* and *podomatic.com* are reliable and representative of a number of available sites. *NOTE: The best practice is to either use the created URL as a link in your class webpage or embed the given player directly into your page so that students won't need to go outside of your site to access the podcast.*

Option B: Become a blogger. Blogging syndication is a popular form for podcasters. Blogs automatically have built-in RSS feeds that can support your podcast. Bloggers create accounts, then upload posts. The blogging software pulls all the needed information from the blog and generates an RSS feed. Most blogging sites and software have added the ability to link a podcast to a blog. At the time of publication, the following blogging sites are reliable: *blogger.com* (general blogging site); *wordpress.com* (general blogging site); *edublog.org* (teacher blogging site); *learnerblogs.org* (student blogging site).

When using Option B, take these steps after creating the podcast:

1. Upload your MP3 file to your server (a school site or an outside provider). You must know the URL where your MP3 file is located.

2. Create a blog account.

3. Go to your blog and make a post. The post title will be the title of the podcast episode. The content of the post will be a description of the podcast.

4. Finally, add a link to the URL of your podcast.

Step 4 Promotion: Does Anyone Know We're Out There?

Recording and uploading a podcast to the Internet is not enough. If you want to have your podcast heard, publicity is the key! This is your chance to share these podcasts with the school and community. Be sure you are happy with the content and quality of your podcast before doing any publicity. If you wait until after the third or fourth episode to advertise, you'll have a better quality podcast and will be likely to attract more return listeners. The steps are simple:

- **Create a podcast blog** for show notes, images, descriptions, and links mentioned during the broadcast. Provide a space on the blog for listeners to post comments about each show.

- **Add subscription buttons** on your website so listeners can subscribe to the RSS podcast feed. They will be able to subscribe to your podcasts using a podcatcher software program. (You can learn about free podcatchers on the Internet.)

- **Publicize** your podcast by emailing a press release to make parents and other educators aware of the show. Include a catchy title, the author's name, a short description of the content, and the location at which listeners can subscribe to the podcast.

- **Submit** your content to the larger podcast directories. Two directories to consider are iTunes® and The Education Podcast Network. Complete a "podcast directories" search to see what sites are avaliable online that might fit your needs. The more sites that list a link to your podcast, the more your podcast will be heard. (Before your submission to iTunes, make sure your RSS feed has all the required iTunes tags.)

- **Submit your site to aggregators.** Aggregators are services that take RSS content from a variety of sites, collect it, and re-organize it into customized formats.

- **Send the URL of your podcast** to several major search engines. Use accurate keywords to attract searchers.

- **Consider burning podcast show CDs,** or saving the MP3 files on flashdrives, to give to parents or others who are not podcast listeners, or who are not tech savvy, so they can listen to the show.

1-2-3-4-Podcast!

Follow this checklist to create your podcast.

Step 1—Pre-Production: Plan, Plan, and Plan

____ Equipment gathered

____ Recording/editing software chosen:

____ Web space identified:

____ Content topic(s) or goals:

____ Format chosen:

____ Outline or script created

____ Music and sound chosen

____ Presentation practiced

Step 2—Production: Quiet on the Set!

____ Settings and equipment tested

____ First take recorded

____ First take edited

____ Music and other sounds added

____ File saved

Step 3—Post-Production: Welcome to Cyberspace!

____ Production uploaded

Describe the method and location:

Step 4— Promotion: Does Anyone Know We're Out There?

___ Publicity plans outlined and implemented

Describe the strategies:

Name _____ Date_____

Podcast Ideas for the Classroom

As students create podcasts, the level of engagement, the caliber of products, and the sophistication of skills will increase—because the audience has now moved beyond the classroom to the world! Whatever topic, content area, or format you choose, remember to keep the focus on your curriculum objectives.

General Podcast Ideas

Parenting Tip: A segment wherein where the counselor or others could offer advice for parents (students could also offer advice or insights) on such topics as "How to Help Kids Succeed with Homework" or "How to Stay Connected to Your Kids"

A Note from the Principal: A weekly podcast wherein the principal shares something (Character Education, Happenings of the Week, Famous Quotes)

Study Tips: A podcast created for parents and students to help them discover how best to study

A School Tour: A tour for new students to see and hear about the school

Library Tours: A tour of the features and basics of the media center and all it has to offer

Audio Newsletter (Class or School): An audio newsletter with all the bells and whistles added to the familiar paper newsletter

Student(s) of the Week: A different student in the spotlight every week so that students can learn more about each other

Book Buddy Read-along: A read-along podcast that works like a "book buddy" for younger kids. (The older student reads the book aloud, pausing to comment on the story and ask prediction questions.)

Field Trip Podcast: A podcast that groups of students make as they participate in a class field trip

Classroom Rules: "Advice to the Next Class" using humor but also expressing to the new students what they need to know about the classroom

Top Ten Tips to Success in Our Classroom: A teacher-created podcast (or a student-created podcast) in a "Top Ten List" format through which the teacher explains what students can do to be successful in the classroom

Character Education: Student-created plays or scenarios in which they demonstrate different character qualities

Podcast Ideas for Instruction, Review, or Reinforcement

Music Lessons: Students practice performances with an accompaniment podcast.

Whole Lessons: Record whole lessons to replay for absent students or students who need reinforcement of specific concepts or skills.

Quiz Show Reviews: Create podcast quiz reviews that students can listen to at home as they study. The format could be "cheesy" and should include dramatic pauses so that students can form their own answers before the correct answer is given.

Living History: Find relatives or community members who have lived through historical moments and interview them (Great Depression, Vietnam War, first walk on the moon).

Readers' Theater: Classes create a readers' theater performance on podcast.

Parody Productions: Create a class or group parody imitating or commenting on a book, article, TV show, movie, or other performance, and produce it on a podcast or video-enhanced podcast.

Comics Come to Life: Create comics that demonstrate learning objectives; then have students create skits and voices to act them out.

Historic Happenings: Students create radio shows where they are "on location" for historical moments (such as electricity is discovered, at the Battle of Gettysburg, reading of the *Declaration of Independence*).

Historic Interviews: Students take roles of either the famous person or the interviewer and then create a script for an interview from the past.

Book Talks: Students create informative book reviews or book talks on a chosen book.

Test Review: Create an audio review to help students prepare for upcoming tests.

So You Want to Be a ___?: Offer career research and presentations in the form of podcasts; could include interviews of professionals along with students' research findings.

Foreign Language Verbal and Listening Skills: Students practice verbal skills of a foreign language by creating podcasts in that language or by listening and following podcast directions in that language.

Science Experiments: Present student-created podcast labs. Give directions, hypotheses, procedures, and results.

That's Debatable: Create a student debate or argumentative speech on podcast, or have students agree or disagree with opinion-based articles on subjects of high interest.

Raps or Songs: Students create and record a song or rap to help with memorization or understanding of any topic or concept that needs to be memorized or reinforced.

Standardized Quiz Format: Create a quiz-style show using standardized test-style questions.

Follow the Campaign Trail: Students create a week-by-week podcast following the candidates and the campaign trail of any local or national election.

Points of Information: Break lessons into short podcast segments (3–7 minutes) in which you lecture on major events or concepts, such as causes of the Civil War, in a simple, straightforward way. Students then select the portion of the lecture that they need to review for reinforcement without listening to the entire 45-minute lecture again.

Tutorials: Build a library of teacher- or student-created step-by-step tutorials for any subject or concept.

Reinforce English Language Learning: Skills can be taught in the native language and students can listen as reinforcement of the concept, or English language help can be recorded as a podcast so students can listen repeatedly for mastery.

Reflections on Learning: Students can create reflection podcasts to solidify what was learned during the lesson.

Direction to Projects: The teacher or students create a podcast of step-by-step directions for a classroom project.